Microsoft Office Specialist Certification

Do you **KNOW ENO**... to **PASS** the exam?

Take a **FREE** online test on the site:

www.testoffice.com

Free practice tests are available directly over the Internet at www.testoffice.com

Don't leave it to chance!

Microsoft® Office XP

EXCEL 2002
Core

Copyright - Editions ENI – February 2002
ISBN: 2-7460-0199-3
Original edition: 2-7460-1423-8

Editions ENI

BP 32125
44021 NANTES Cedex 1

Tél. 02.51.80.15.15
Fax 02.51.80.15.16

e-mail : editions@ediENI.COM
http://www.editions-eni.com

English edition by Adrienne TOMMY

Collection directed by Corinne HERVO

MOUS
Excel 2002 Core

INTRODUCTION 3

WORKBOOKS AND WORKSHEETS

1.1 Workbooks 13
1.2 Worksheets 33

ROWS, COLUMNS AND CELLS

2.1 Rows/Columns 43
2.2 Cells 53

MANAGING DATA

3.1 Entering data 61
3.2 Finding and editing data 77
3.3 Copying and moving 97
3.4 Filters 109
3.5 Sharing data through a Web site 115

CALCULATIONS

4.1 Formulas 131
4.2 Functions 141

PRESENTATION OF DATA

5.1 Formatting data.. 155

5.2 Styles.. 177

PRINTING

6.1 Printing 183

6.2 Page Setup 193

DRAWING OBJECTS

7.1 Charts... 203

7.2 Drawing objects.. 223

SUMMARY EXERCISES... 241

TABLE OF OBJECTIVES 250

INDEX.. 253

This logo is your guarantee that you are using a Microsoft® approved preparation guide for the Microsoft® Office User Specialist Excel 2002 Core exam.

This complete preparation guide provides you with the theory that explains all the features tested in the exam and practical exercises that you can work through, to find out how much you really know. When you can work through all these exercises, successfully and easily, you are ready to take the MOUS exam. At the end of the book, there is a list of all the Excel 2002 Core exam objectives and the lesson number and exercise that relate to each objective.

For further information on the titles in the MOUS collection, visit the ENI Publishing Web site, at **www.eni-publishing.com**; click the **Catalogue** link then click the **MOUS** link in the list of ENI collections.

What is the MOUS certification?

The MOUS (Microsoft Office User Specialist) exam gives you the opportunity to obtain a meaningful certification, recognised by Microsoft®, for the Office applications: Word, Excel, Access, PowerPoint, and Outlook. This certification guarantees your level of skill in working with these applications. It can provide a boost to your career ambitions, as it proves that you can use effectively all the features of the Microsoft Office applications and thus offer a high productivity level to your employer. In addition, it is a certain plus when job-seeking: more and more companies require employment candidates to be MOUS certificate holders.

What are the applications concerned?

You can gain MOUS certification in Word 97 and Excel 97 as well as the Office 2000 and Office XP applications: Word, Excel, Access, Powerpoint and Outlook. For Word 97 and Excel 97, only one level exists. However, there are two levels available for Word 2000, Excel 2000, Word 2002 and Excel 2002, consisting of a Core level, for basic skills, and an advanced Expert level. If you obtain the Expert level for Word and Excel as well as MOUS certification in PowerPoint, Access and Outlook (Office 2000 or XP), you are certified as a Master.

How do you apply to sit the exams?

To enrol for the exams, you should contact one of the Microsoft Authorized Testing Centers (or ATC). A list of these centres is available online at this address: http://www.mous.net. Make sure you know the version of the Office application for which you wish to obtain the certificate (is it the 97, 2000 or 2002 version?).

There is an enrolment fee for each exam.

On the day of the exam, you should carry some form of identification and, if you have already sat a MOUS exam, your ID number.

What happens during the MOUS exam?

During the exam, you will have your own computer, on which you must perform a series of set tasks in the application concerned. Each action required to perform each task is tested, to ensure that you have done exactly what you were asked to do.

You are allowed no notes, books, pencils or calculators during the exam. You can consult the application help, but you should be careful not to exceed the exam's time limit.

Each exam is timed; it lasts in general between 45 minutes and one hour.

How do you pass the exam?

You must carry out a certain percentage of the required tasks correctly, within the allocated time. This percentage varies depending on the exam.

You will be told your result as soon as you have finished your exam. These results are confidential (the data are coded) and are made known only to the candidate and to Microsoft.

What happens then?

You will receive a Microsoft-approved exam certificate, proving that you hold the specified MOUS (Microsoft Office User Specialist) level.

What happens if I fail?

You can take the exam as many times as you like, but will have to pay the enrolment fee again each time you apply.

How this book works

This book is the ideal companion to an effective preparation of the **MOUS Excel 2002 Core** exam. It is divided into several sections, each containing one or more **chapters**. Each section deals with a specific topic: managing workbooks and worksheets, modifying rows, columns and cells in a table, entering and editing text and values, making various calculations, formatting a table, printing, creating drawing objects and charts. Each chapter is independent from the others. You can tailor the training to suit you: if you already know how to format data, for example, you can skip this lesson and go straight to the practice exercise for that chapter, then if you feel you need some extra theory, you can look back at the relevant points in the lesson. You can also study the lessons and/or work through the exercises in any order you wish.

At the end of the book, there is an **index** to help you find the explanations for any action, whenever you need them.

From theory...

Each chapter starts with a **lesson** on the theme in question, made up of a variable amount of numbered topics. The lesson should supply you with all the theoretical information necessary to acquire that particular skill. Example screens to illustrate the point discussed enhance the lesson and you will also find tips, tricks and remarks to complement the explanations provided.

...To practice

Test your knowledge by working through the **practice exercise** at the end of each chapter: each numbered heading corresponds to an exercise question. A solution to the exercise follows. These exercises are done using the documents on the CD-ROM accompanying the book, that you install on your own computer (to see how, refer to the INSTALLING THE CD-ROM instructions). In addition to the chapter exercises, seven **summary exercises** dealing with each of the section themes are included at the end of the book. The solutions to these exercises appear as documents on the CD-ROM.

All you need to succeed!

When you can complete all the practice exercises without any hesitation or problems, you are ready to sit the MOUS exam. In the table of contents for each chapter, the topics corresponding to a specific exam objective are marked with this symbol: ▦. At the back of the book, you can also see **the official list of the Excel 2002 Core exam objectives** and for each of these objectives the corresponding lesson and exercise number.

Free online training

Editions ENI have developed a series of practice tests for the MOUS exams. These tests are free and can be found on the www.moustest.com site. These tests take place online, within the application in question, just like in the official exam. To use this, you need an Internet connection on your computer, the application (e.g. Word 2000) and Internet Explorer 5.0 or later. At the end of the test, you can see your results in detail.

The layout of this book

This book is laid out in a specific way with special typefaces and symbols so you can find all the information you need quickly and easily:

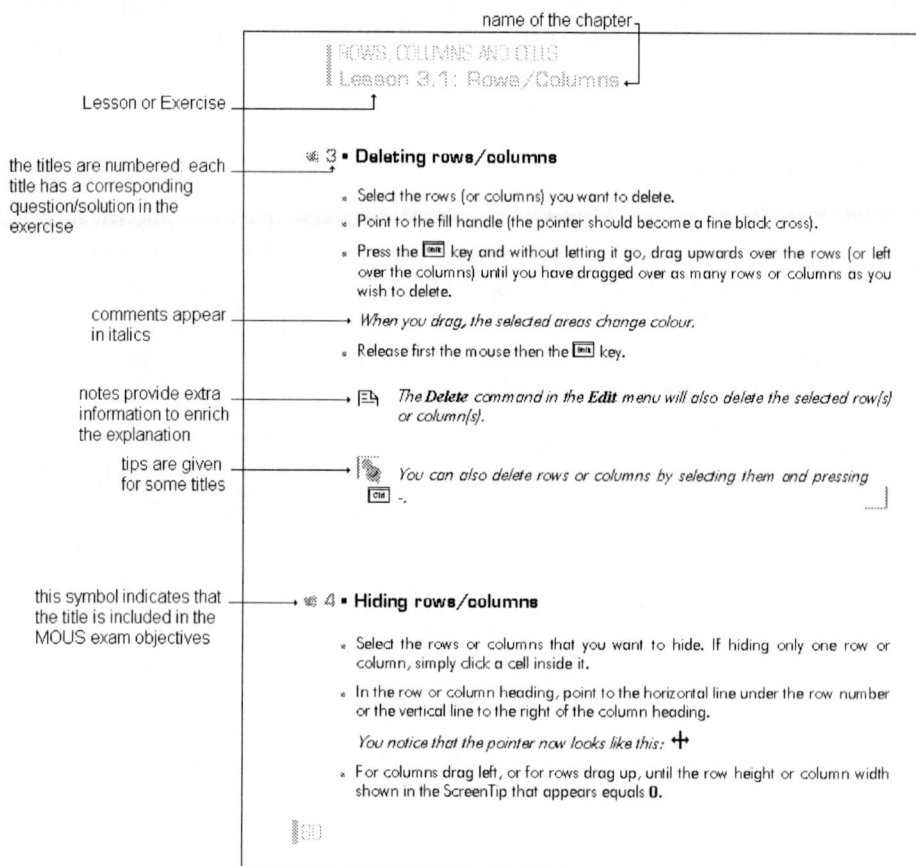

name of the chapter

ROWS, COLUMNS AND CELLS
Lesson 3.1: Rows/Columns

Lesson or Exercise

the titles are numbered: each title has a corresponding question/solution in the exercise

3 • Deleting rows/columns

» Select the rows (or columns) you want to delete.
» Point to the fill handle (the pointer should become a fine black cross).
» Press the [Shift] key and without letting it go, drag upwards over the rows (or left over the columns) until you have dragged over as many rows or columns as you wish to delete.

comments appear in italics

When you drag, the selected areas change colour.

» Release first the mouse then the [Shift] key.

notes provide extra information to enrich the explanation

*The **Delete** command in the **Edit** menu will also delete the selected row(s) or column(s).*

tips are given for some titles

You can also delete rows or columns by selecting them and pressing [Ctrl] -.

this symbol indicates that the title is included in the MOUS exam objectives

4 • Hiding rows/columns

» Select the rows or columns that you want to hide. If hiding only one row or column, simply click a cell inside it.
» In the row or column heading, point to the horizontal line under the row number or the vertical line to the right of the column heading.

You notice that the pointer now looks like this: ✛

» For columns drag left, or for rows drag up, until the row height or column width shown in the ScreenTip that appears equals **0**.

You can tell whether an action should be performed with the mouse, the keyboard or with the menu options by referring to the symbol that introduces each action: 🖰, ⬨ and 🗐.

Installing the CD-ROM

The CD-ROM provided contains the documents used to work through the practice and summary exercises and the summary exercise solutions. When you follow the installation procedure set out below, a folder called MOUS Excel 2002 is created on your hard disk and the CD-ROM documents are decompressed and copied into the created folder. The CD-ROM also contains a template which you should copy into the Excel Templates folder.

- Put the CD-ROM into the CD-ROM drive of your computer.

- Start the Windows Explorer: right-click the **Start** button and choose the **Explore** option.

- In the left pane of the Explorer window, scroll through the list until the CD-ROM drive icon appears. Click this icon.

The contents of the CD-ROM appear in the right pane of the Explorer window. The documents used for the practice and summary exercises are compressed in the MOUS Excel 2002.exe file, although they also exist in standard form in the Practice Exercises and Summary folders.

- Double-click the icon of the **MOUS Excel 2002** folder in the right pane of the Explorer window.

*The **MOUS Excel 2002** dialog box appears.*

- Click **Next**.

The installation application offers to create a folder called MOUS Excel 2002.

- Modify the proposed folder name if you wish then click **Next**. If several people are going to be doing the practice exercises on the same computer, you should modify the folder name so each person will be working on his/her own copy of the folder.

- Click **Yes** to confirm creating the **MOUS Excel 2002** folder.

The installation application decompresses the documents then copies them into the created folder.

- Click **Finish** when the copying process is finished.

  You must now copy the templates into the templates folder used by Excel. Depending on the version of Windows you are using, the default file path to this Templates folder can vary. For Windows 98 and Me, the path is generally C:\Windows\Application Data\Microsoft\Templates, and for Windows 2000 Professional and XP the path is usually C:\Documents and Settings\user_name\ Application Data\Microsoft\Templates.

- If you are not working in Windows 2000 Professional or XP, you can go directly to the next point. Otherwise, use the **Tools - Folder Options** command in the Windows Explorer, click the **View** tab and activate the **Show hidden files and folders** option, which ensures that the entire hierarchy of files on your computer appears (this is not always the case in Windows 2000 and XP).

- Click the template called **1-1 Aztec Charter.xlt** in the right pane of the Explorer.

- Open the **Edit** menu then click the **Copy** option to copy the template into the Windows clipboard.

- If necessary, scroll through the contents of the left pane of the window until you can see the **Windows** folder or **Documents and Settings**, depending on your version of Windows. Click the plus (+) sign to the left of the folder to see a list of the folders it contains.

  The + sign becomes a - sign.

- Click the + sign to the left of each subfolder, following the stated file path until you reach the **Templates** folder.

  By default, the templates are stored in this folder.

- Use the **Edit - Paste** command to copy the contents of the clipboard into the **Templates** folder.

- This file, copied directly from the CD-ROM, is a read-only file, which means it cannot be modified. As you need to work on this file for one of the exercises, you will need to remedy this problem. To do this, select the template, then right-click the selection and take the **Properties** option. Deactivate the **Read only** option and confirm with **OK**.

* If you are using Windows 2000 Professional or XP, you can, if you wish, deactivate the **Show hidden files and folders** option in **Tools - Folder Options - View** tab of the Windows Explorer.

* When the copy is finished, click the ☒ button on the **Explorer** window to close it.

   You can now put away the CD-ROM and start working on your MOUS exam preparation.

WORKBOOKS AND WORKSHEETS
Lesson 1.1: Workbooks

1 ▪ Opening a workbook.. 14

2 ▪ Displaying/hiding an open workbook 17

3 ▪ Creating a new workbook 17

4 ▪ Creating a workbook based on a template.................. 17

5 ▪ Saving a workbook.. 19

6 ▪ Saving a workbook under another name...................... 21

7 ▪ Creating a folder 21

8 ▪ Choosing the default file location............................... 22

9 ▪ Saving a sheet/workbook as a Web page.................... 22

10 ▪ Previewing a Web page in Excel.................................. 27

Practice Exercise 1.1 28

1 ▪ Opening a workbook

» **File - Open** or ⌷ or [Ctrl] **O**

*You can also click the **More workbooks** link on the **New Workbook** task pane.*

» To indicate where the document to be opened is located, click one of the buttons on the **Places Bar** (on the left side of the dialog box) or open the **Look in** drop-down list.

*The **History** button lets you view the 50 most recently used documents and/or folders. The **My Documents** button shows the contents of the **My Documents** folder. The **Desktop** shows the shortcuts installed on the Windows Desktop. The **Favorites** button opens the **Favorites** folder.*

*Depending on your version of Windows, you will have a **My Network Places** button, to view all your network shortcuts, or a **Web Folders** button, to create or access folders installed on Web servers.*

*The **Look in** list contains all the accessible drives on your computer (the floppy drive (A :), the hard drive (C :), perhaps a CD-ROM drive) and on your local network (My Network Places).*

» Select the drive where the document is stored (A:, C:, D:, etc.) if it is on your workstation or click the **My Network Places** button to go to a network location.

» Go to the folder containing the workbook you want to open by double-clicking its icon; open any subfolders in the same way.

» To go to the folder above, click the ⌷ button.

» Click the ⌷ button to return to folders you have already used.

» To view a detailed file list, open the list on the ⌷ button then click ⌷.

*In this view, the name of each workbook appears in the first column and the list also displays the document's **Size**, its **Type** and the time and date of its last modification.*

■ To display the properties of a selected workbook, open the drop-down list on the ▦ ▾ button, click ▦ then choose the workbook whose properties you wish to see.

*Certain properties such as the title, subject, or comments appear only if details of the workbook have been entered in the **File - Properties** dialog box, on the **Summary** page.*

■ To see the contents of a given workbook, open the list on the ▦ ▾ button then click ▦ and select the name of the workbook concerned.

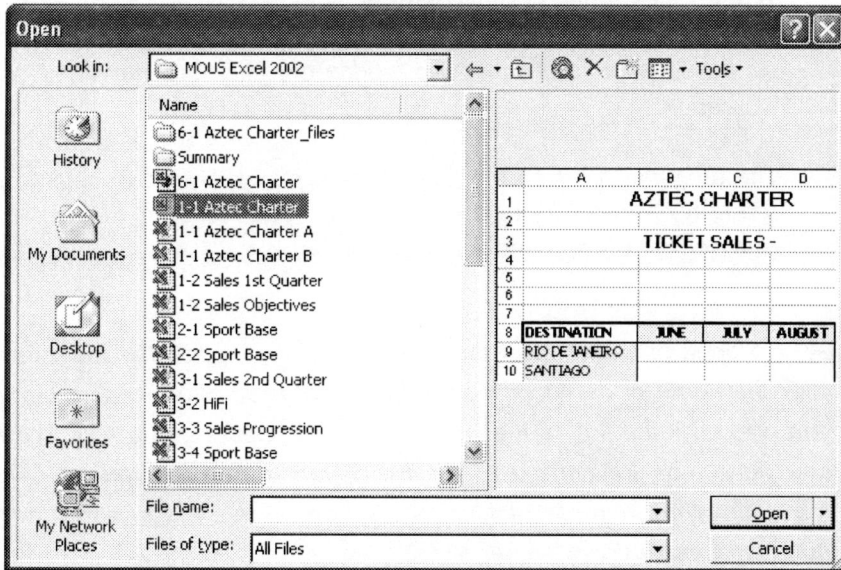

*A preview picture of the selected workbook appears in the right pane of the dialog box, providing you activated the **Save preview picture** option in **File - Properties - Summary** tab the last time you used and saved the workbook.*

■ To display only the names of the workbooks and their associated icons, open the ⊞ ▼ list and click ▦ to use a list presentation style. Click ▯ to show the list of workbooks with large icons or ▯ to show them as small icons.

■ To open a workbook, select it then click **Open** or double-click its name.

■ To open several workbooks at once, select them using ⇧[Shift]-clicks if the files are adjacent or [Ctrl]-clicks if they are not adjacent in the file list. Click **Open** to open the selected workbooks.

📄 *To activate a workbook which is open but hidden, click its name in the* ***Window*** *menu (the active workbook has a tick by its name). If the* ***Windows in Taskbar*** *option is active in* ***Tools - Options - View*** *tab, a button appears on the taskbar for each open workbook; click the button to activate the workbook.*

The drop-down list on the ***Open*** *button allows you to open a workbook in read-only mode, to open a copy, to open certain files in the default browser, or to open and repair a workbook.*

🔍 *To open one of the last four workbooks used, open the* ***File*** *menu and click the name of the workbook in the list at the bottom of the menu. You can also click the link to the workbook that appears in the* ***New Workbook*** *task pane. The* ***Recently used file list*** *option in* ***Tools - Options - General*** *tab defines the number of files listed (from 1 to 9); you can modify the number of* ***entries***.

2 ▪ Displaying/hiding an open workbook

» On the taskbar, click the button of the workbook you want to activate.

*You can also **Hide** or **Unhide** an open workbook by choosing the corresponding option in the **Window** menu.*

The open workbooks are listed in alphabetical order at the bottom of this menu. The active workbook is the one that is ticked.

» Click the workbook's name to activate it.

3 ▪ Creating a new workbook

» **File - New** or ⬜ or ⌊Ctrl⌋ **N**

» Click the **Blank Workbook** link in the **New Workbook** task pane.

*If the **New Workbook** task pane is already on display, simply click the **Blank Workbook** link, without using the **File - New** command.*

*A new workbook, called **BookX**, appears. This workbook is based on the default template.*

4 ▪ Creating a workbook based on a template

» If necessary, use the **File - New** command to show the **New Workbook** task pane.

```
◄ ◄  New Workbook          ▼ ✕
Open a workbook
        1-1 Aztec Charter B
        1-1 Aztec Charter A
        Staff schedules
        Exam results
     📂 More workbooks...
New
     ▯ Blank Workbook
New from existing workbook
     🖼 Choose workbook...
New from template
     🗔 General Templates...
     🌐 Templates on my Web Sites...
     🌐 Templates on Microsoft.com


     📁 Add Network Place...
     ❓ Microsoft Excel Help
     ☑ Show at startup
```

⁂ Click the **General Templates** link in the **New from template** section.

*The templates located in the **Templates** folder (cf. Installing the CD-ROM) appear on the **General** page and the predefined templates supplied with Excel appear on the **Spreadsheet Solutions** page (these are generally saved in C:\Program Files\Microsoft Office\Templates\1036.*

⁂ If necessary, click the tab that corresponds to the group of templates you wish to see.

⁂ Double-click the template name.

When you open a template, Excel copies its contents into a new workbook; this workbook takes the template name, followed by a number.

⁂ Enter the information into the new workbook.

⁂ Save this new workbook as you would save any ordinary one.

📄 *When you have created a workbook from a template, the template's name appears as a link in the **New from template** section on the **New Workbook** task pane. You can now click the link to create a new workbook based on that template.*

*The **Templates on my Web Sites** and **Templates on Microsoft.com** links in the **New from template** section on the **New Workbook** task pane take you to Web sites so you can download other templates.*

*If you decide to create a workbook based on a predefined Excel template, you may see a message telling you that the corresponding component is not installed. If this happens, insert the installation CD-ROM and click **Yes** to install the component.*

5 ▪ Saving a workbook

A new workbook

▪ **File - Save** or 💾 or ⌨ Ctrl **S**

▪ Using the **Save in** drop-down list, choose the drive in which you want to save the workbook; you can also use one of the icons on the **Places Bar**.

▪ Go into the folder where you want to save the workbook by double-clicking the folder icon.

▪ Double-click the **File name** text box then enter the name you want to give to the workbook: you can use up to 255 characters, including spaces.

* Click the **Save** button.

The workbook name appears on the title bar: Excel workbooks take an .xls extension (which may not necessarily be visible).

An existing workbook

* **File - Save** or [icon] or [Ctrl] **S**

If you are closing a workbook or leaving Excel, you may want to click the cell that should be active the next time the document is opened, before you save it.

🪟6 ▪ Saving a workbook under another name

⊛ Open the workbook that you want to duplicate by using **File - Open** or 📂 or ⌊Ctrl⌋ **O**.

⊛ Make any changes required in the workbook.

⊛ **File - Save As**

⊛ Select the drive, then the folder in which the workbook should be saved, using the **Save in** list or the **Places Bar**.

⊛ In the **Save as type** list, select, if necessary, the format in which the file should be saved.

You can for example save a workbook in xml format.

⊛ Enter a new file name in the **File name** text box.

⊛ Click the **Save** button.

The changes made to the workbook are saved only in the copy and it is this copy that now appears on the screen.

🪟7 ▪ Creating a folder

It is possible that when you save a workbook, the folder in which you want to save it may not exist. You can create a new folder directly from Excel.

⊛ **File - Save** or **File - Save As**

⊛ Using the **Save in** list or the **Places Bar**, select the drive then the folder in which you wish to create a new folder.

⊛ Click the 📁 tool button.

- Enter the **Name** for the folder in the corresponding box.

- Click **OK**.

- Close the dialog box by clicking the ⊠ button or save the active workbook by clicking the **Save** button.

📄 *You can also create a folder within the **Open** dialog box (**File - Open**).*

▦8 ▪ Choosing the default file location

This is the file location that Excel will offer you automatically whenever you save or open a workbook.

- **Tools - Options - General** tab

- In the **Default file location** box, give the path of this default folder.

- Click **OK**.

▦9 ▪ Saving a sheet/workbook as a Web page

Saving a non-interactive Web page

*A **non-interactive Web page** contains information saved in Web (html) format, that can be consulted by users visiting your Internet/intranet site but cannot be modified. You can save a selection of cells, a worksheet or a whole Excel 2002, workbook in html format, without added interactivity.*

- Create or open the workbook you want to save as a Web page.

- If necessary, select the data concerned, or make no selection if you are saving the entire workbook or the active sheet.

- **File - Save as Web Page**

- Select the location in which you want to publish your Web page, using the **Save in** list or the **Places Bar**. Depending on your version of Windows, the **Places Bar** can take you rapidly to one of the previously created **Web Folders** (in Windows NT 4.0/98) or to the existing **My Network Places** (in Windows 2000/Me/XP).

- Use the **Web Options** in the **Tools** menu to modify the settings for the Web page you are publishing, such as the standard browser, published file management, encoding, fonts and so on.

- Specify what you are saving by activating the appropriate option; the **Entire Workbook**, certain cells (**Selection: [cell range]**) or the active sheet (**Selection: Sheet**).

  *The name of the **Selection** option changes, depending on whether a selection was made or not.*

- Make sure the **Add Interactivity** option is not active.

- If you wish, click the **Change Title** button and enter the text that will appear on the browser's title bar when the Web page is opened, then click **OK** to confirm.

- If necessary, change the proposed **File name**.

  You should avoid putting spaces and accents in file names.

- Click the **Save** button.

  *The Web page appears in Excel in html format and the original file closes automatically. Along with the Web page, Excel generates a folder that contains all the components of the Web page, which are called "supporting files". This supporting files folder is called **Web page name_files**; it cannot be dissociated from the Web page.*

Saving an interactive Web page

A visitor to an Excel interactive Web page can modify the presentation and values of data in the page. Changes made in this way are not carried over to the source file and are not saved.

⁌ Create or open the workbook that you want to publish; you can publish either a whole workbook or a sheet.

⁌ If you want to save only one sheet in the workbook as a Web page, activate the sheet by clicking its tab.

⁌ **File - Save as Web Page**

⁌ Select the location in which you want to publish your Web page, using the **Save in** list or the **Places Bar**. Depending on your version of Windows, the **Places Bar** can take you rapidly to one of the previously created **Web Folders** (in Windows NT 4.0/98) or to the existing **My Network Places** (in Windows 2000/Me/XP).

⁌ Use the **Web Options** in the **Tools** menu to modify the settings for the Web page you are publishing, such as the standard browser, published file management, encoding, fonts and so on.

⁌ Select the **Selection: Sheet** or **Entire Workbook** option, according to what you wish to save, and tick the **Add Interactivity** check box.

⁌ If necessary, click the **Change Title** button to enter the text that will appear in the browser's title bar when you open the Web page then click **OK**.

⁌ If you wish, modify the suggested **File name**.

You should avoid putting spaces and accents in file names.

⁌ Click the **Save** button.

The Web page is created in html format. For an interactive Web page, Excel does not generate a supporting files folder.

To view an interactive Web page, you must open it directly in your Web browser.

The features available for modifying the Web page's layout and contents vary, depending on whether the Web page corresponds to a whole workbook or just a worksheet.

Here is an example of an <u>interactive worksheet</u>:

The above example shows the result of publishing the active sheet that contains a PivotTable, with added interactivity. You can see that each field (such as Region) has a drop-down list attached, containing the details of that field. It is possible to tick or deactivate one or more items to modify the values displayed in the PivotTable. A visitor to this page could change the presentation of the table, using the various tools on offer. He/she does not even need to have the Excel application installed, as all the modifications are performed directly in the Web browser (however, he/she does need to have the appropriate Microsoft licence to use these Excel features).

Here is an example of an _interactive workbook:_

The example above shows the result of publishing an entire workbook, with one of the worksheets (called Analysis) containing a PivotTable. You notice that the visitor to this type of page cannot intervene in the same way as the interactive worksheet shown in the previous illustration: here, the fields are fixed, there are fewer tools available and so on. However, the visitor can display and work on the sheet of his/her choice, by clicking the down arrow on the sheet tab at the bottom left of the table and choosing the name of the required sheet.

📄 To delete a Web page, use the Windows Explorer to go to the server and/or folder where the Web page is located. Select the Web page (file_name.htm) and its supporting files folder (filename_files), if you are deleting a saved non-interactive Web page. Press the ⌈Del⌋ key and click the **Yes** button to confirm the deletion.

10 ▪ Previewing a Web page in Excel

▪ Open the non-interactive Web page (htm file) that you wish to preview.

To preview an interactive Web page, you should open it directly in your Web browser.

▪ **File - Web Page Preview**

The default browser (for example, Microsoft Internet Explorer) opens and presents the Web page as it would be seen on the Internet and/or an intranet. The Excel application and the htm file stay open.

▪ Once you have finished looking at the preview, close the browser window by clicking its ☒ button.

Below, you can see **Practice Exercise** 1.1. This exercise is made up of 10 steps. If you do not know how to do one of the steps, go back to the title that corresponds to that particular lesson. When you have finished, you can check your work by reading the **Solution** that follows.

Steps that are likely to be tested during the MOUS exam are marked with this symbol: ▦. However, it is a good idea to complete the whole exercise to ensure you have understood everything covered in the lesson.

☞ **Practice Exercise 1.1**

▦ 1. Open the **1-1 Aztec Charter A.xls** and **1-1 Aztec Charter B.xls** workbooks located in the **MOUS Excel 2002** folder.

2. Display the **1-1 Aztec Charter B.xls** workbook on the screen.

3. Create a new workbook.

▦ 4. Create a new workbook based on the **1-1 Aztec Charter.xlt** template.

5. Save the new workbook based on the **1-1 Aztec Charter.xlt** template in the **MOUS Excel 2002** folder. You can call this workbook **1-1 Aztec Charter C.xls**.

▦ 6. In the **MOUS Excel 2002** folder, save the **1-1 Aztec Charter C.xls** workbook under the name **1-1 Aztec Charter Sales Objectives**.

▦ 7. In the **MOUS Excel 2002** folder, create a new folder called **Web Pages**.

▦ 8. Make the **C:\MOUS Excel 2002** folder your default working folder (if necessary, replace C: by the name of the hard disk on which you saved this folder).

9. Display the **1-1 Aztec Charter B.xls** workbook on the screen then save it as a Web page in the **Web Pages** folder. You do not have to change the document name.

10. Starting from the Excel application, preview the **1-1 Aztec Charter B.htm** Web page in a browser.

If you want to put what you have learnt into practice on a real document, you can work on summary exercise 1 for the WORKBOOKS AND WORKSHEETS section, that you can find at the end of this book.

WORKBOOKS AND WORKSHEETS
Exercise 1.1: Workbooks

It is often possible to perform a task in several different ways, but here, only the easiest solution is presented. You can go back to the corresponding lesson if you want to see other techniques you could use.

Solution to Exercise 1.1

1. To open the **1-1 Aztec Charter A.xls** and **1-1 Aztec Charter B.xls** workbooks, located in the **MOUS Excel 2002** folder, click the ⬀ button, open the **Look in** drop-down list then select the disk drive into which you copied the documents from the CD-ROM provided with this book.

   Double-click the **MOUS Excel 2002** folder, click the **1-1 Aztec Charter A.xls** file then hold down the `Ctrl` key and click the **1-1 Aztec Charter B.xls**.

   Click the **Open** button.

2. To display the **1-1 Aztec Charter B.xls** workbook on the screen, click the button on the taskbar that corresponds to the **1-1 Aztec Charter B.xls** workbook.

3. To create a new workbook, click the ▯ tool button.

4. To create a new workbook based on the **1-1 Aztec Charter.xlt** template, use the **File - New** command and on the **New Workbook** task pane, click the **General Templates** link. On the **General** page, double-click the **1-1 Aztec Charter.xlt** icon.

5. To save the new workbook created from the **1-1 Aztec Charter** template, click the ⊞ tool button.

Open the **Save in** drop-down list, select the disk drive in which the **MOUS Excel 2002** folder is located then double-click the **MOUS Excel 2002** folder to open it.

Enter **1-1 Aztec Charter C** in the **File name** text box. Click the **Save** button.

6. To save the **1-1 Aztec Charter C.xls** workbook in the **MOUS Excel 2002** folder under the name of **1-1 Aztec Charter Sales Objectives**, use the **File - Save As** command.

Open the **Save in** drop-down list, select the drive in which the **MOUS Excel 2002** folder is stored and double-click the folder icon.

Leave **Microsoft Excel Workbook (*.xls)** in the **Save as type** box then enter **1-1 Aztec Charter Sales Objectives** as the **File name**. Finish by clicking the **Save** button.

7. To create a new folder within the **MOUS Excel 2002** folder called **Web Pages**, use the **File - Save As** command.

Open the **Save in** drop-down list, select the drive where the **MOUS Excel 2002** folder is located and double-click its icon.

Click the ⊞ tool button, enter **Web Pages** then click **OK** on the **New Folder** dialog box.

Close the **Save As** dialog box by clicking the ☒ button.

8. To set the C:\MOUS Excel 2002 folder as your default working folder, use the **Tools - Options** command and click the **General** tab. In the **Default file location** text box, enter the name of the folder concerned (**C:\ MOUS Excel 2002**) and click **OK** to confirm.

9. To save the **1-1 Aztec Charter B.xls** workbook as a Web page, start by displaying it: click the **1-1 Aztec Charter B.xls** button on the taskbar.

Choose the **File - Save as Web Page** command.

Select the drive containing the **MOUS Excel 2002** folder and double-click its icon, then double-click the **Web Pages** folder.

Leave the **Entire Workbook** option active, do not change the **File name** and make sure the **Add Interactivity** option is not active. Click the **Save** button.

10. To preview the 1-1 Aztec Charter B.htm Web page in your browser, starting from the Excel application, display the **1-1 Aztec Charter B.htm** workbook in Excel, if it is not already on display, then use the **File - Web Page Preview** command.

WORKBOOKS AND WORKSHEETS
Lesson 1.2: Worksheets

1 ▪ Moving around in a worksheet.. 34

2 ▪ Moving from one sheet to another... 35

3 ▪ Naming a sheet 35

4 ▪ Changing the colour of the worksheet tab................................ 36

5 ▪ Moving a sheet within a workbook 36

6 ▪ Copying a sheet in a workbook.. 36

7 ▪ Moving/copying a sheet from one workbook to another.......... 37

8 ▪ Deleting sheets.. 38

9 ▪ Inserting sheets 38

Practice Exercise 1.2 39

WORKBOOKS AND WORKSHEETS
Lesson 1.2: Worksheets

1 ▪ Moving around in a worksheet

You can choose between several techniques, depending on which tool you want to use: the mouse or the keyboard.

🖱 ▪ Use the scroll bars to move the sheet until you see the cell you want to activate:

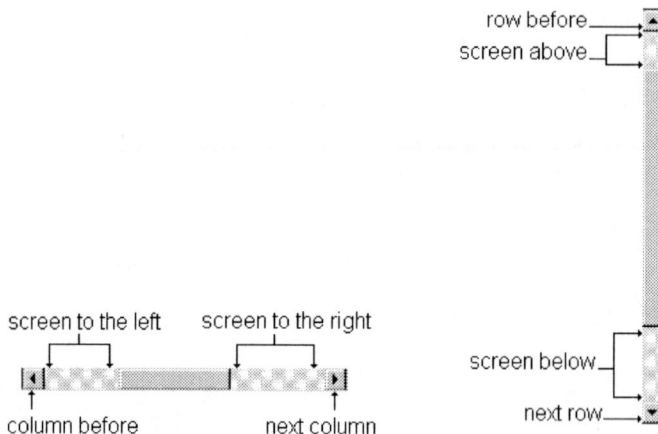

row before
screen above

screen to the left   screen to the right

column before   next column

screen below

next row

When you drag the scroll cursor, a ScreenTip appears, showing the row number or column letter currently reached.

⬢ ▪ Use the keyboard in the following way:

to go to the cell on the right	→ or ⭾
to go to the cell on the left	← or Shift ⭾
to go up one cell	↑ or Shift ↵
to go down one cell	↓ or ↵
to go to the screen on the right	Alt PgDn
to go to the screen on the left	Alt PgUp
to go up one screen	PgUp
to go down one screen	PgDn
column A of the active row	Home
cell A1	Ctrl Home

34

» To go to a specific cell, double-click the **Name Box** on the left of the formula bar, type in the cell reference then enter.

2 ▪ Moving from one sheet to another

At the bottom of each worksheet, Excel shows the tabs of all the sheets it contains so you can identify them. The name of the active sheet appears in bold type on a white tab.

» Using the tab scroll buttons, scroll the sheet tabs until you can see the one where you want to go.

```
                            first tab
                            previous tab
                            next tab
                            last tab

  I◄  ◄  ►  ►I \ City Bookshop / Between the Covers / Chart - ◄
  Ready
```

» Click the tab of the sheet that you want to see.

📄 *You can also use the* Ctrl PgDn *and* Ctrl PgUp *keys to go to the next sheet and the previous sheet, respectively.*

3 ▪ Naming a sheet

This name appears on the sheet tab.

» Double-click the tab of the sheet you want to rename.

» Type the new name over the sheet's previous name.

This name cannot contain more than 31 characters (including spaces). It should not be placed between brackets, nor contain these characters: colon (:), slash (/), backslash (\), question mark (?) or asterisk (*).

» Press ↵ to confirm.

▣4 ▪ Changing the colour of the worksheet tab

- Go to the sheet concerned, or if necessary select several worksheets by holding down ⌈Shift⌉ and clicking the tabs.

- **Format - Sheet - Tab Color**

- Click the colour of your choice.

- Click **OK**.

  The colour of the selected sheet(s) appears on the tab as a coloured line beneath the tab's name, when the sheet is active. When it is inactive, the whole tab is coloured.

▣5 ▪ Moving a sheet within a workbook

- Click the tab you want to move.

- Drag this tab into its new position.

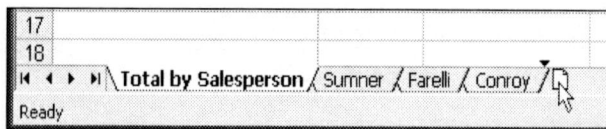

- When you are satisfied with the sheet's position, you can release the mouse button.

6 ▪ Copying a sheet in a workbook

- Click the tab of the sheet you want to copy.

- While holding down the ⌈Ctrl⌉ key, drag to the position in which you want to place the copy of the sheet.

- When you are satisfied with the sheet's position, release the mouse button.

7 ▪ Moving/copying a sheet from one workbook to another

- ❊ Open the workbook containing the sheet you wish to transfer and the destination workbook.

- ❊ Go into the sheet you want to move/copy.

- ❊ **Edit - Move or Copy Sheet**

- ❊ Open the list called **To book** and click the name of the destination workbook.

- ❊ In the **Before sheet** list box, select the sheet in the destination workbook in front of which you want to insert the other sheet.

- ❊ Activate, if necessary, the **Create a copy** option.

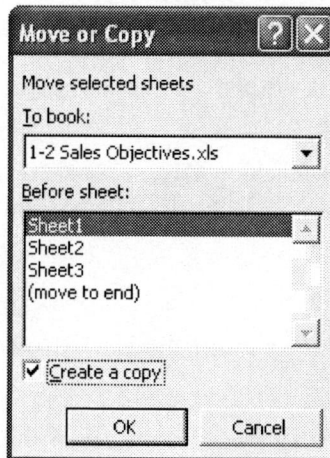

- ❊ Click **OK**.

   The destination workbook becomes the active workbook.

⊞8 ▪ Deleting sheets

- Select the sheets you wish to delete. If they are adjacent, click the first tab, hold down the ⊞Shift key and click the last; if they are non-adjacent, hold down ⊞Ctrl and click each sheet tab concerned.

- **Edit - Delete Sheet**

> Microsoft Excel ⊠
>
> ⚠ Data may exist in the sheet(s) selected for deletion. To permanently delete the data, press Delete.
>
> [Delete]   [Cancel]

If the Office Assistant is visible, this confirmation prompt will appear in a pale yellow ScreenTip.

- Confirm your request by clicking **OK**.

⊞9 ▪ Inserting sheets

- Decide where you want to insert the new sheet and select the sheet that will come after it.

- To insert several sheets at once, hold down the ⊞Shift key and select as many sheet tabs as you want to insert new sheets.

- **Insert - Worksheet**

Below you can see **Practice Exercise** 1.2. This exercise is made up of 9 steps. If you do not know how to do one of the steps, go back to the title that corresponds to that particular lesson. When you have finished, you can check your work by reading the **Solution** that follows.

Steps that are likely to be tested during the MOUS exam are marked with this symbol: ▦. However, it is a good idea to complete the whole exercise to ensure you have understood everything covered in the lesson.

☞ Practice Exercise 1.2

*To work on exercise 1.2, you should open the **1-2 Sales 1st Quarter.xls** workbook located in the **MOUS Excel 2002** folder*

1. Using the keyboard, show the **Sheet1** worksheet on the screen then return to cell **B7** in the **Total by Salesperson** sheet.

2. Display the contents of **Sheet2** on the screen, using the mouse.

▦ 3. Name **Sheet1** as **Sumner**, **Sheet2** as **Farelli**, and **Sheet3** as **Conroy**.

▦ 4. Apply the colour **yellow** to the **Sumner**, **Farelli** and **Conroy** sheet tabs.

▦ 5. Move the **Total by Salesperson** sheet after the **Conroy** sheet.

6. Insert a copy of the **Total by Salesperson** sheet in front of the **Sumner** sheet.

7. Place a copy of the **Sumner** sheet in front of the **Sheet1** sheet in the **1-2 Sales Objectives.xls** workbook, located in the **MOUS Excel 2002** folder.

   Close the **1-2 Sales Objectives.xls** workbook, saving your changes when prompted.

8. Delete the first worksheet in the **1-2 Sales 1st Quarter** workbook, called **Total by Salesperson (2)**.

9. Insert a worksheet between the **Conroy** and **Total by Salesperson** sheets and call it **Thompson**.

If you want to put what you have learnt into practice on a real document, you can work on summary exercise 1 for the WORKBOOKS AND WORKSHEETS section that you can find at the end of this book.

It is often possible to perform a task in several different ways, but here, only the easiest solution is presented. You can go back to the corresponding lesson if you want to see other techniques you could use.

Solution to Exercise 1.2

1. To display the **Sheet1** worksheet on the screen, using the keyboard, press Ctrl PgDn. To return to cell **B7** in the **Total by Salesperson** sheet, press Ctrl PgUp.

2. To display the contents of **Sheet2** on the screen with the mouse, click the **Sheet2** tab.

3. To rename the **Sheet1** sheet as **Sumner** double-click the **Sheet1** tab, type **Sumner** then confirm by pressing ↵.

   To rename the **Sheet2** sheet as **Farelli**, double-click the **Sheet2** tab, type **Farelli** then confirm by pressing ↵.

   To rename the **Sheet3** sheet as **Conroy**, double-click the **Sheet3** tab then type **Conroy** and confirm by pressing ↵.

4. To apply a yellow colour to the Sumner, Farelli and Conroy sheet tabs, select the **Sumner**, **Farelli** and **Conroy** sheet tabs by holding down Ctrl and clicking them. Use the **Format - Sheet - Tab Color** command, click the yellow colour swatch and confirm with **OK**.

5. To move the Total by Salesperson sheet to the right of the Conroy sheet, click the **Total by Salesperson** tab and drag it in position to the right of the **Conroy** tab.

6. To make a copy of the Total by Salesperson sheet and move it in front of the Sumner sheet, click the **Total by Salesperson** tab then hold down the `Ctrl` key and drag this tab in front of the **Sumner** tab.

7. To make a copy of the Sumner sheet and place that copy in front of the Sheet1 sheet in the 1-2 Sales Objectives.xls workbook, first open the **1-2 Sales Objectives.xls** workbook in the **MOUS Excel 2002** folder then return the **1-2 Sales 1st Quarter.xls** workbook to the screen.

   Click the tab of the **Sumner** sheet then use the **Edit - Move or Copy Sheet** command.
   Open the **To book** list and select the **1-2 Sales Objectives.xls** workbook.
   In the **Before sheet** text box, leave **Sheet1** selected.
   Activate the **Create a copy** option then click **OK**.

   Close the **1-2 Sales Objectives.xls** workbook by clicking the ☒ button on the workbook window then click the **Yes** button when prompted to save the changes made.

8. To delete the first worksheet in the workbook, called Total by Salesperson (2), click the **Total by Salesperson (2)** tab then use the **Edit - Delete Sheet** command.
   Click **Delete** to confirm this deletion.

9. To insert a worksheet between the Conroy and Total by Salesperson sheets, click the **Total by Salesperson** tab and use the **Insert - Worksheet** command.

   To name the sheet you have just inserted, double-click its tab, type **Thompson** then confirm by pressing ↵.

ROWS, COLUMNS AND CELLS
Lesson 2.1: Rows/Columns

1 ▪ Selecting rows/columns 44

2 ▪ Inserting rows/columns.. 44

3 ▪ Deleting rows/columns... 45

4 ▪ Hiding/showing rows/columns 46

5 ▪ Freezing/unfreezing rows and/or columns..................................... 46

6 ▪ Changing column width/row height 47

7 ▪ Adjusting columns/rows to fit contents... 48

Practice Exercise 2.1 49

ROWS, COLUMNS AND CELLS
Lesson 2.1: Rows/Columns

1 ▪ Selecting rows/columns

▪ Use one of the following techniques:

	Row	Column
🖱	click the row number to select it.	click the column letter to select it.
🎲	activate a cell in the required row and press [Shift][Space].	activate a cell in the required column and press [Ctrl][Space].

When a row (or column) is selected, its number (or letter) appears in a dark colour.

To select several adjacent rows or columns, use the mouse to drag over the row or column headings. If the rows or columns are not adjacent, hold down the [Ctrl] key while you select each row or column.

2 ▪ Inserting rows/columns

🖱 ▪ Select the row (or column) after which you wish to insert the new row(s) (or column(s)).

▪ Point to the fill handle.

Make sure the mouse pointer has become a black cross, with no arrowheads on it.

▪ Hold down [Shift] and without releasing the key, drag the fill handle over the same number of rows (or columns) as you want to insert new ones.

When inserting rows you must drag downwards, not upwards, and for columns, drag towards the right (and not left).

▪ Release first the mouse button then the [Shift] key.

As you drag, you notice that you are actually dragging a grey bar.

📄 *With this technique, it is not possible to insert rows before row 1 or columns before column A.*

▤ ▪ Select the row (or column) after which you wish to insert the new row(s) (or column(s)).

To insert several rows or columns, select as many rows/columns as you want to insert new ones.

▪ **Insert - Rows** or **Columns**

📄 *When you insert a row or column, the inserted item adopts the formatting of the row or column previously located there. You can modify this by clicking the **Insert Options** button 🖌 that appears next to the inserted item. In the menu that appears, choose to **Format Same As Above** or **Format Same As Below** (for a row), **Format Same As Right** or **Format Same As Left** (for a column) or to **Clear Formatting** altogether.*

You can also insert a row or column by selecting a row or column (clicking its header) and pressing ⌨Ctrl +.

🏠3 ▪ **Deleting rows/columns**

▪ Select the rows (or columns) you want to delete, by clicking their headers.

▪ Use **Edit - Delete** or right-click the selected row/column and choose **Delete**.

🖱 *You can also delete rows or columns by selecting them and pressing ⌨Ctrl -.*

▥4 ▪ Hiding/showing rows/columns

▪ Select the rows or columns that you want to hide. If you are hiding only one row or column, simply click a cell inside it.

▪ To hide the selected rows/columns, use **Format - Row** or **Column** (or right-click one of the selected row or column headers) and choose the **Hide** option.

▪ To display hidden columns again, select the column to the right and the column to the left of the hidden column(s). To display hidden rows again, select the row above and the row beneath the hidden row(s).

Format - Row or **Column** or right-click one of the selected row or column headers. Click the **Unhide** option.

*This method does not allow you to display a hidden column **A** and/or row **1**. To do that, go to the column or row headers and point to the line to the left of column **B** or above row **2**. Drag this line to the right (to unhide column A) or down (to unhide row 1).*

▥5 ▪ Freezing/unfreezing rows and/or columns

This action fixes certain rows or columns on the screen in order to show two sets of data that are far apart on a worksheet.

▪ To freeze the column that contains the row titles, make sure that this column is the first one which appears on the left of the screen (if you need to freeze more than one column, make sure that the first of them is displayed at the very left of the screen). To freeze the row which contains column titles, make sure that it is displayed right at the top of the screen (if there are several rows to freeze, the first of them should appear at the top).

▪ When the screen is displayed satisfactorily, click a cell in the column after the column(s) you want to freeze and/or click a cell in the row underneath the row(s) you want to freeze.

- **Window - Freeze Panes**

	A	B	D	E	F	G	H	I	J	K
1	Name	First Name	PC/City	Sex	Age	Cat	Subs	Paid		
11	Greene	Louise	5600 St Luc	F	25			Y		
12	Hunt	Rosemary	5000 Gunst	F	18			Y		
13	Loxton	Marie	4400 Mt Gla	F	22			Y		
14	Marsh	Sarah	6000 Lorton	F	19			Y		
15	Martingale	Joanne	4500 Greent	F	19			Y		
16	Norton	Vera	4100 Tewes	F	24			Y		
17	Peak	Alison	4200 New G	F	21			Y		
18	Peyton	Theresa	4400 Mt Gla	F	25			N		
19	Rowe	Patricia	4400 Mt Gla	F	15			N		
20	Sanders	Heather	6100 Hersto	F	12			N		
21	Smith	Liza	4500 Greent	F	12			N		

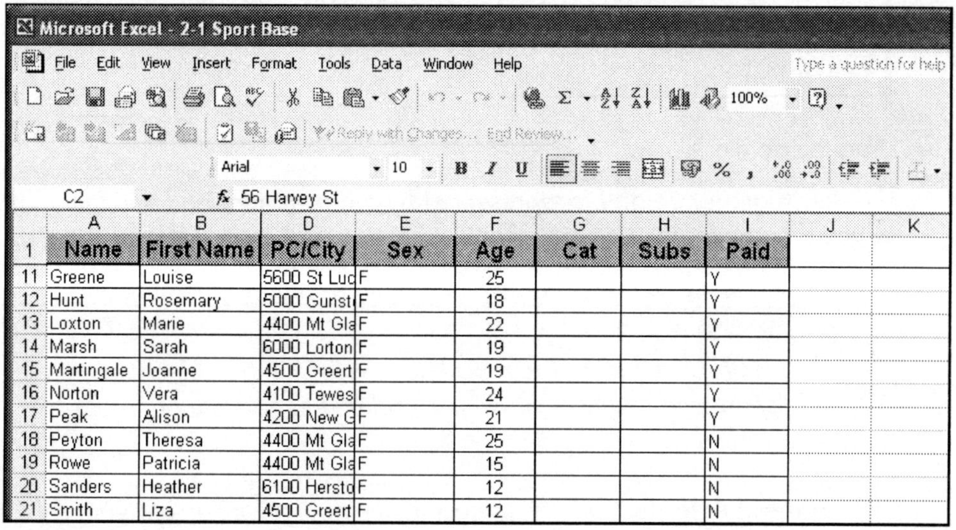

Here, columns A and B have been frozen, as has row 1. You can see that when the sheet is scrolled, column D appears next to column B and row 11 is below row 1.

To release titles that have been frozen, use ***Window - Unfreeze Panes****.*

6 • Changing column width/row height

- Select each column that should have the same width (or each row that should be the same height). If only one row or column is involved, do not select it, merely click any cell inside it.
- Point to the vertical line on the right of one of the selected column headings (or the horizontal line below one of the selected row numbers).

You can see that the pointer has changed shape.

* Drag the pointer.

The new width (or height) is represented by a dotted line, and the value reached as you drag appears in a ScreenTip.

* Release the mouse when you reach the required width (or height).

The width of a column is calculated as a number of characters (and in pixels) and the height of a row is calculated in points (and in pixels).

*You will save memory by using this method to space out your tables, rather than inserting new rows or columns. To modify the selected column width/row height in a very precise manner, you can use the **Format - Row** or **Column - Width** or **Height** command.*

7 ▪ Adjusting columns/rows to fit contents

When you activate this feature, the column width is then calculated according to the longest cell entry in the column and the row height according to the highest cell entry in the row.

* To adjust column width, double-click the vertical line to the right of the letter of the column in question.
To adjust row height, double-click the horizontal line under the number of the row in question.

Below you can see **Practice Exercise** 2.1. This exercise is made up of 7 steps. If you do not know how to do one of the steps, go back to the title that corresponds to that particular lesson. When you have finished, you can check your work by reading the **Solution** that follows.

Steps that are likely to be tested during the MOUS exam are marked with this symbol: ⊞. However, it is a good idea to complete the whole exercise to ensure you have understood everything covered in the lesson.

☞ **Practice Exercise 2.1**

*To work on exercise 2.1, you should open the **2-1 Sport Base.xls** workbook in the **MOUS Excel 2002** folder.*

1. Select columns **A**, **B**, **E** and **F**.

⊞ 2. Insert three rows after row **6** and one column after column **C**.

⊞ 3. Delete rows **7**, **8** and **9** as well as column **D**.

⊞ 4. Hide columns **C** and **D**, then display them again.

⊞ 5. Freeze the titles in columns **A** and **B** as well as the titles in row **1**.

⊞ 6. Increase the width of column **C** to **23** and height of row **1** to **21**.

7. Adjust columns **D** and **E** to fit their contents.

If you want to put what you have learnt into practice on a real document, you can work on summary exercise 2 for the ROWS, COLUMNS AND CELLS section that you can find at the end of this book.

It is often possible to perform a task in several different ways, but here, only the easiest solution is presented. You can go back to the corresponding lesson if you want to see other techniques you could use.

Solution to Exercise 2.1

1. To select columns A, B, E, et F, drag the pointer over the column headings **A** and **B**, hold down the ⌈Ctrl⌋ key then drag the pointer again from column heading **E** to **F**.

2. To insert three rows after row **6**, select row **6** then point to the fill handle. While holding down the ⌈Shift⌋ key, drag the fill handle down over three rows.

   To insert a column after column **C**, select column **C** then point to the fill handle.
   While holding down the ⌈Shift⌋ key, drag the fill handle to the right over one column.

3. To delete rows 7, 8 and 9, select rows **7, 8** and **9** then press ⌈Ctrl⌋ -.
   To delete column **D**, select column **D** then press ⌈Ctrl⌋ -.

4. To hide columns C and D, select columns **C** and **D** then use the **Format - Column - Hide** command.

   To unhide columns C and D, select columns **B** and **E** then use the **Format - Column - Unhide** command.

5. To freeze the titles in columns **A** and **B** and those in row **1**, click in cell **C2** then use the **Window - Freeze Panes** command.

6. To increase the width of column C to 23, point to the vertical line to the right of the column heading **C**.
Drag to the right then release the mouse button when the value in the ScreenTip reads **23**.

To increase the height of row 1 to 21, point to the horizontal line underneath the number of row **1**.
Drag downwards then release the mouse button when the value in the ScreenTip reads **21**.

7. To adjust the width of columns D and E to fit their contents, select columns **D** and **E** then double-click the vertical line on the right of the column **E** heading.

ROWS, COLUMNS AND CELLS
Exercise 2.1: Rows/Columns

ROWS, COLUMNS AND CELLS
Lesson 2.2: Cells

1 ▪ Selecting adjacent cells 54

2 ▪ Selecting non-adjacent cells 54

3 ▪ Selecting all the cells in a sheet 55

▦ 4 ▪ Going to a specific cell 55

5 ▪ Selecting cells according to content 56

▦ 6 ▪ Inserting empty cells 57

▦ 7 ▪ Moving cells then inserting them 57

▦ 8 ▪ Deleting cells 57

Practice Exercise 2.2 58

ROWS, COLUMNS AND CELLS
Lesson 2.2: Cells

1 ▪ Selecting adjacent cells

※ Use one of the following three techniques:

Dragging   Click the first cell you want to select then, holding down the mouse button, drag the mouse over the other cells. When you are satisfied with the selection, you can release the mouse button.

Be careful not to drag the fill handle (the black square in the bottom right corner of the active cell)!

[Shift]-clicking   Click the first cell to be selected and then point to the last cell concerned. Hold down [Shift] and click; release the mouse button then the key.

Using the keyboard   Hold down the [Shift] key and use the appropriate arrow keys to select the required cells.

	A	B	C	D	E
	Name	First Name	Address	PC/City	Sex
	Alderman	Christine	56 Harvey St	4100 Tewesbury	F
	Andrews	Melissa	27 Ridley St	5600 St Lucia	F
	Barnett	Frances	38 Harrison Cres	4500 Greerton	F
	Charles	Yolanda	29 Bartlett Cres	6000 Lorton	F
	Cray	Hannah	77 Kennedy Drive	5800 Rafter	F
	Dell	Tammy	13 Read Road	4300 Dryden	F
	Dorcas	Michelle	10 Kings Ct	5400 Fern Grove	F

The selected **cell range** *appears in a darker colour except for the first cell, which is the active cell and appears like a normal cell.*

📄   *By default, the status bar shows the sum of the values in the selected cells.*

2 ▪ Selecting non-adjacent cells

※ Select the first cell or group of cells.

※ Point to the first cell in the next group.

Remember, point but do not click yet!

* Hold down the [Ctrl] key and if necessary, drag to select several cells.

* Release the [Ctrl] key first then the mouse button.

📄 *In a formula or in a dialog box, a selection of non-adjacent cells is represented by a comma. For example: A5:A10,L5:L10 represents the cell ranges A5 to A10 and L5 to L10.*

3 ▪ Selecting all the cells in a sheet

* Click the button located at the intersection of the column containing the row numbers and the row containing the column letters or press [Ctrl] [Shift] [Space] or [Ctrl] **A**.

4 ▪ Going to a specific cell

* Click in the **Name Box** on the left of the formula bar where the address of the active cell is displayed.

A4	▼	*fx* Barnett	
	A	B	C
1	**Name**	**First Name**	**Address**
2	Alderman	Christine	56 Harvey St
3	Andrews	Melissa	27 Ridley St
4	Barnett	Frances	38 Harrison Cres
5	Charles	Yolanda	29 Bartlett Cres
6	Cray	Hannah	77 Kennedy Drive
7	Dell	Tammy	13 Read Road

The reference of the active cell is selected.

* Enter the reference of the cell where you want to go.

* Confirm by pressing ↵.

You can also go to a specific cell using the **Edit - Go To** command (Ctrl **G**); in the **Reference** text box, enter the reference of the cell where you want to go then click **OK**.

5 ▪ Selecting cells according to content

» **Edit - Go To** or F5 or Ctrl **G**

» Click the **Special** button.

» Choose the type of cell you want to select.

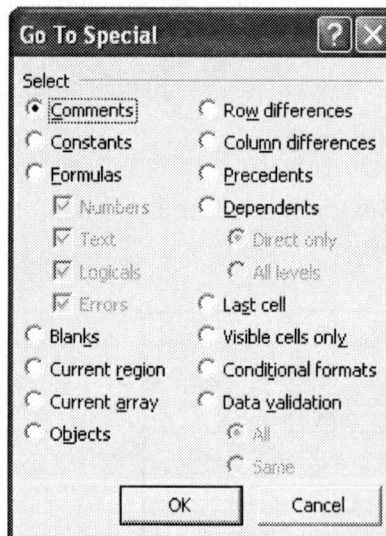

» Click **OK**.

📖6 ▪ Inserting empty cells

🖱 ▪ Select the cell <u>that comes before</u> the place you wish to insert the new cells.

   ▪ Hold down [Shift] and drag the fill handle over as many cells as you want to insert new ones.

📑 ▪ Select as many cells as you want to insert of new ones.

   ▪ **Insert - Cells** or [Ctrl] **+**

   ▪ Activate the first or second option to indicate how the existing cells should move to make way for the new ones.

   ▪ Click **OK**.

📖7 ▪ Moving cells then inserting them

   The cells are moved and inserted between other existing cells.

   ▪ Select the cells you want to move.

   ▪ Point to one of the edges of the selected range.

   ▪ Hold down the [Shift] key and drag the selected cells.

   ▪ Release the mouse when you reach the point where the cells will be inserted, symbolised by a thick hatched line, then release the [Shift] key.

📖8 ▪ Deleting cells

   ▪ Select the cells you want to delete.

   ▪ Hold down the [Shift] key and drag the fill handle up over the selection.

   📄 *Deleting in this way moves the remaining cells upwards. If you want the remaining cells to be moved to the left, use the **Edit - Delete** command or use the [Ctrl] - keys.*

Below, you can see **Practice Exercise** 2.2. This exercise is made up of 8 steps. If you do not know how to do one of the steps, go back to the title that corresponds to that particular lesson. When you have finished, you can check your work by reading the **Solution** that follows.

Steps that are likely to be tested during the MOUS exam are marked with this symbol: ▦. However, it is a good idea to complete the whole exercise to ensure you have understood everything covered in the lesson.

☞ Practice Exercise 2.2

To work on exercise 2.2, you should open the **2-2 Sport Base.xls** workbook in the **MOUS Excel 2002** folder.

1. Select cells **A2** to **B47**.

2. Select cells **E2** to **F47** and **I2** to **I47**.

3. Select all the cells on the worksheet.

▦ 4. Go to cell **C45**.

5. Go to the blank cells in the list of data.

▦ 6. Insert three empty cells underneath cell **D4**.

▦ 7. Move cell **C7** and insert it between cells **C8** and **C9**.

▦ 8. Delete cells **D5** to **D7**.

If you want to put what you have learnt into practice on a real document, you can work on summary exercise 2 for ROWS, COLUMNS AND CELLS section, that you can find at the end of this book.

It is often possible to perform a task in several different ways, but here, only the easiest solution is presented. You can go back to the corresponding lesson if you want to see other techniques you could use.

Solution to Exercise 2.2

1. To select cells A2 to B47, click in cell **A2** then hold down the mouse button and drag the mouse to cell **B47**.

2. To select cells E2 to F47 and I2 to I47, start by selecting the range of cells **E2** to **F47**.
   Point to cell **I2** then hold down the [Ctrl] key and select the cell range **I2** to **I47**.

3. To select all the cells on the worksheet, press [Ctrl] **A**.

4. To go to cell C45, click the **Name Box** on the left of the formula bar where the reference of the active cell is displayed.
   Type **C45** then press ↵ on the keyboard.

5. To select the empty cells in the data list, use the **Edit - Go To** command and click the **Special** button.
   Activate the **Blanks** option then click **OK**.

6. To insert three empty cells below cell D4, click cell **D4** to select it.
   Hold down the [Shift] key and drag the fill handle downward over three cells.

7. To move cell C7 and insert it between cells C8 and C9, click cell **C7** to select it.

   Point to one of the edges of cell **C7** then hold down the ⌈Shift⌉ key. Drag the selected cell between cells **C8** and **C9**: the place where the cells will be inserted is symbolised by a thick hatched line.

   Release the mouse button then the ⌈Shift⌉ key.

8. To delete cells D5 to D7, select them.

   Point to the fill handle then hold down the ⌈Shift⌉ key and drag the fill handle upwards over cells **D7** to **D5**.

   Release the mouse button then the ⌈Shift⌉ key.

MANAGING DATA
Lesson 3.1: Entering data

1 ▪ Entering constants 62

2 ▪ Entering several lines of text in one cell 65

3 ▪ Creating a series of data 66

4 ▪ Creating a custom data series 68

5 ▪ Creating a hyperlink 69

6 ▪ Calculating values from different sheets 72

Practice Exercise 3.1 73

▤1 ▪ Entering constants

Entering text, values, dates

▪ Activate the cell where you want to display the data.

*You should always check the active cell reference in the **Name Box** on the left of the formula bar.*

▪ Enter the data.

B7	▾ X ✓ *fx* 4185		
	A	B	C	D
1	TOTAL SALES PER SALESPERSON			
2				
3				
4	SALESPEOPLE			
5		5680	5290	5284
6		4575	4796	4400
7		4185		4050	5125
8	TOTAL	14440	14136	14809
9		5680	5290	5284
10				

Once you have entered the first character, two symbols appear in the formula bar:

☒   *to cancel the entry (corresponds to the* Esc *key).*

☑   *to confirm the entry (corresponds to the* ⏎ *key).*

At the same time, the word «Enter» appears on the status bar to indicate that only data entry can be performed.

▪ Activate the next cell where you wish to enter data or press ⏎.

The act of going to a new cell confirms the previous entry. Once you activate a new cell (with the mouse or using one of the arrow keys), Excel returns to Ready mode and the ☒ *and* ☑ *symbols disappear.*

Once confirmed, *Text type data are left aligned in the cells, and Date or Number type data are aligned on the right of the cells. In addition to this, Date type data are formatted (for example, 12/01 becomes 12-Jan or 01-Dec, depending on your computer's regional settings).*

■ Continue with your other data entry.

*It is essential to confirm the last item entered so you can return to **Ready** mode.*

■ When entering data, you should keep the following observations in mind:

- You can type up to 32767 characters of text in each cell.

- With numerical data, be careful to type in 0 (zero) and not O (the letter o).

- Negative values can be indicated by either preceding them with a minus sign (-) or by placing them within brackets.

- If you enter £10000 or $10000, Excel immediately applies a £10,000 or $10,000 format.

- To enter a percentage, type a % sign just after the number.

- To enter decimals, use a decimal point as separator (this should be the decimal separator specified in your Windows Regional Settings).

📄 *When dates are entered, Excel interprets years entered as two numbers in this way:*
- from 00 to 29 as the years 2000 to 2029,
- from 30 to 99 as the years 1930 to 1999.

*Number, currency, date and time settings depend on your operating system and can be modified in **Control Panel - Regional Settings** (or **Regional Options** or **Regional and Language Options**, depending on your version of Windows), under the **Date** or **Regional Options** tab.*

Inserting symbols

This technique inserts symbols that do not appear on your keyboard. A symbol can be inserted in an empty cell or within text while you are entering it.

- **Insert - Symbol - Symbols** tab
- In the **Font** list, select the font that contains the character you want to insert.
- Select the required character.

- Click the **Insert** button.
- Close the dialog box with the **Close** button that appears.

Entering the system date

※ Activate the cell where you want to display the date.

※ There are three ways to insert the computer's current date:

=TODAY()   Inserts the current system date, which is updated each time the sheet is opened.

=NOW()   Inserts the current system date and time, which are updated when the sheet is opened.

[Ctrl] **;**   Inserts the current system date, but it will not be updated automatically.

※ Enter.

📄 *If the date displayed is incorrect, you should correct your computer's system date.*

2 ▪ Entering several lines of text in one cell

※ Activate the cell that you want to fill in.

※ Enter the cell contents, pressing [Alt ↵] whenever you want to insert a line break.

A9	▾ ✗ ✓ fx	BEST		
	A	RESULT		
9	**RESULT**	5680	5290	5284
10				
11				
12	Table created:	03/02/2002		
13				

※ Press ↵ to confirm.

📄 *The **Wrap text** option (**Format - Cells - Alignment** tab) also uses several lines to display the contents of a cell but Excel defines the line breaks automatically to fit the text to the column.*

3 ▪ Creating a series of data

A series is a logical progression of cell values. You can create a series of dates, times, months, days or a combination of text and numerical values.

Creating a simple series

A simple series shows a list of values, incrementing each time by one value.

* Enter the first value in the series.

* Drag the fill handle from the bottom right of that cell to the last target cell for the series.

	SALESPEOPLE	APRIL	MAY	JUNE	
3					
4	SALESPEOPLE	APRIL	MAY	JUNE	
5		5680	5290	5284	
6		4575	4796	4400	
7		4185	4050	5125	
8	TOTAL	14440	14136	14809	
9	BEST RESULT	5680	5290	5284	
10					

* When you reach the end of your series, the **Auto Fill Options** button appears to the bottom right of the series. If you click this button, you can (depending on the type of series, and your needs) choose an option to modify the way the values are copied or incremented.

	SALESPEOPLE	APRIL	MAY	JUNE	
3					
4	SALESPEOPLE	APRIL	MAY	JUNE	
5		5680	5290	5284	
6		4575	4796	4400	○ Copy Cells
7		4185	4050	5125	● Fill Series
8	TOTAL	14440	14136	14809	○ Fill Formatting Only
9	BEST RESULT	5680	5290	5284	○ Fill Without Formatting
10					○ Fill Months
11					

Creating a complex series

With this type of series, you can define the interval between each value.

- Enter the first two values, to give an indication of the interval you want to use.
- Select these two cells.
- Drag the fill handle.

	Inches	Centimetres
1		
2	**METRIC CONVERSION**	
3		
4	Inches	Centimetres
5	1	2.54
6	2	5.08
7	3	7.62
8	4	10.16
9	5	12.70
10	6	15.24
11		
12		

Here, the interval value of 2.54 is repeated over the whole series.

- Enter the first value in the series then select the cell containing that value.
- **Edit - Fill - Series**

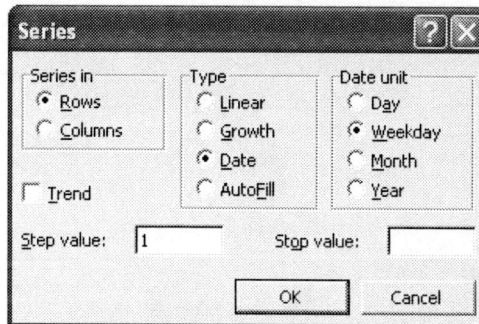

Series

Series in	Type	Date unit
● Rows	○ Linear	○ Day
○ Columns	○ Growth	● Weekday
	● Date	○ Month
□ Trend	○ AutoFill	○ Year

Step value: 1   Stop value: [   ]

[OK]   [Cancel]

- In the **Series in** frame, indicate whether the series should be inserted in **Rows** or **Columns**.

- In the **Type** frame, specify the type of series you are making.
- If you choose a **Date** type, give the **Date unit** in the right hand frame.
- Modify the **Step value** as necessary.
- Indicate the **Stop value** (the last value) in the series.
- Click **OK**.

4 ▪ Creating a custom data series

- **Tools - Options - Custom Lists** tab
- In the **Custom lists** box, click **NEW LIST** even if this choice has already been selected.

  *The insertion point appears in the **List entries** box.*

- In the **List entries** box, enter each item of data, separating each by pressing ⏎.

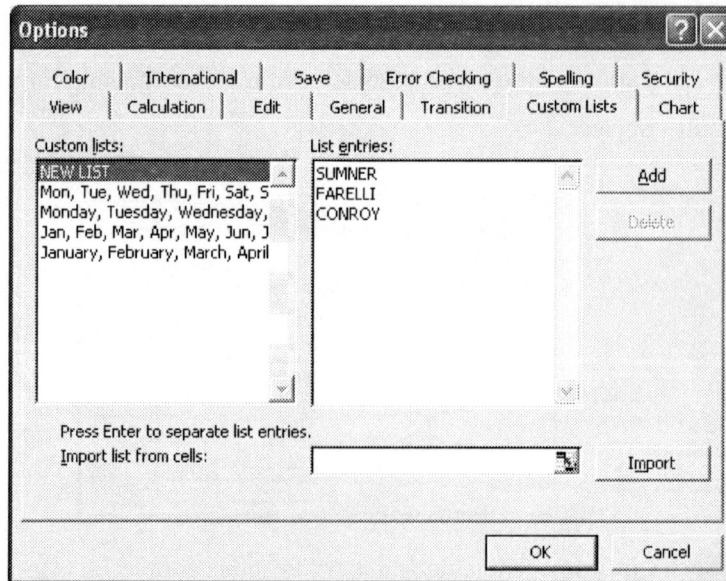

» Click the **Add** button.

The new list appears among the current custom lists: each entry is separated from the previous one by a comma.

» Press **OK** to confirm.

» To insert a custom data series, click the first required cell and enter one of the list values. Drag the fill handle from the active cell to the cell where the last value is to be shown.

⊞5 ▪ Creating a hyperlink

Creating a hyperlink towards an existing file or Web page

» Select the cell where you wish the hyperlink to be placed.

» **Insert - Hyperlink** or 🔲 or ⌈Ctrl⌉ **K**

» If necessary, activate the **Existing File or Web Page** shortcut in the left part of the dialog box.

» According to your needs, activate one of the shortcuts in the centre of the dialog box (**Current Folder, Browsed Pages, Recent Files**).

» If you are creating a link to an item in the **Current Folder**, you can use the **Look in** list to select the drive in which the workbook is stored then double-click the folder (and any subfolders) to get to the workbook to which you wish to create the link.

» Whether you chose to create a hyperlink to a **Current Folder**, one of the **Browsed Pages**, or one of the **Recent Files**, go to the central part of the dialog box and choose the Web page or workbook to which you want to establish your link. You can also enter the complete **Address** of the item concerned, in the text box of the same name.

This document can be either a document located on a workstation drive or an Internet address.

- If necessary, click the **ScreenTip** button and enter the text that should appear when you point to the link. If you do not do this, Excel will display the hyperlink's address in the ScreenTip.

- To access a particular place in the document directly, use the **Bookmark** button and select the name of the item you want to go to. If necessary, modify the link name that will appear in the cell.

  You can use the name of a worksheet, a range of named cells and so forth.

- Click **OK** to create the link.

Creating a hyperlink to a specific place within a workbook

- Select the cell in which you wish to insert the hyperlink.

- **Insert - Hyperlink** or ou [Ctrl] **K**

- Click the **Place in This Document** shortcut on the **Link to** bar on the left of the dialog box.

  The list of existing sheets and the named ranges defined in the active workbook appear in the central part of the dialog box.

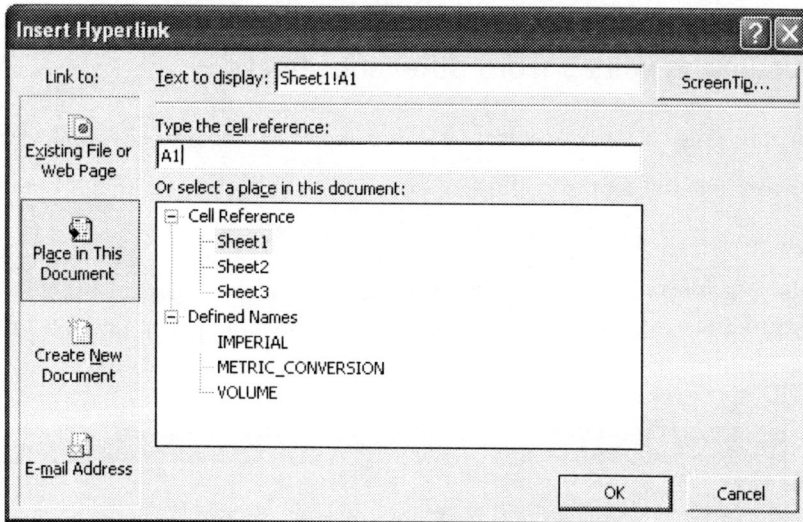

- In the **Or select a place in this document** list, click the name of the worksheet or the defined name to which you want to establish the link.

- **Type the cell reference** for the cell concerned by the link in the corresponding text box.

- If necessary, click the **ScreenTip** button and enter the **ScreenTip text** that should appear when you point to the link. This text can be a helpful hint, an explanation, an address or a similar item. Confirm with **OK**.

- Click **OK** in the **Insert Hyperlink** dialog box to create the link you have defined.

To activate a hyperlink, simply click it.
To delete a hyperlink, point to the cell concerned then hold down the mouse button (as opposed to a simple click which will follow the link). Press the Del key to delete the link.

6 ▪ Calculating values from different sheets

You can enter a formula into one worksheet that refers to cells on another sheet.

▪ Activate the cell that is going to display the result.

▪ Type =

▪ Enter the formula, selecting the appropriate cells in the worksheet(s) concerned. If you wish to use a cell on another worksheet, click that sheet's tab then click the required cell.

In the formula displayed in the formula bar, the cell's name is preceded by the name of the source sheet. Here, for example, cell **B7** contains a formula that displays the value that is in cell **B10** on the **Conroy** worksheet.

▪ Press ⏎ to confirm.

Below, you can see **Practice Exercise** 3.1. This exercise is made up of 6 steps. If you do not know how to do one of the steps, go back to the title that corresponds to that particular lesson. When you have finished, you can check your work by reading the **Solution** that follows.

Steps that are likely to be tested during the MOUS exam are marked with this symbol: 🖫. However, it is a good idea to complete the whole exercise to ensure you have understood everything covered in the lesson.

👉 Practice Exercise 3.1

To work on exercise 3.1, you should open the **3-1 Sales 2nd Quarter.xls** workbook in the **MOUS Excel 2002** folder then activate the **Sheet1** worksheet.

🖫 1. Enter this text:
   - **TOTAL SALES PER SALESPERSON** in cell **A1**.
   - **4185** in cell **B7**.
   - **3/2/02** in cell **B12**.

2. Enter **Best Result** over two lines in cell **A9**.

3. Create the data series **APRIL**, **MAY** and **JUNE** in cells **B4** to **D4**.

4. Create a custom data series containing the names **SUMNER, FARELLI** and **CONROY**. Insert this list into cells **A5** to **A7**.

🖫 5. In cell **A15**, insert a hyperlink that accesses the **1-2 Sales 1st Quarter.xls** workbook in the **MOUS Excel 2002** folder. Go into that document with the hyperlink.

6. In the **1-2 Sales 1st Quarter.xls** workbook, complete the **Total by Salesperson** worksheet by inserting the sales figures made by **Conroy** in **January**, from the data on the **Conroy** worksheet.

If you want to put what you have learnt into practice on a real document, you can work on summary exercise 3 for the MANAGING DATA section, that you can find at the end of this book.

It is often possible to perform a task in several different ways, but here, only the easiest solution is presented. You can go back to the corresponding lesson if you want to see other techniques you could use.

Solution to Exercise 3.1

1. To enter the text TOTAL SALES PER SALESPERSON into cell A1, click in cell **A1**, type **TOTAL SALES PER SALESPERSON** then confirm with the ⏎ key.

   To enter the value 4185 into cell B7, click cell **B7**, type **4185** then confirm by pressing ⏎.

   To enter the date 3/2/02 into cell B12, click cell **B12**, type **3/2/02** then confirm by pressing ⏎.

2. To enter Best Result over two lines in cell A9, click cell **A9** to select it.
   Type **Best** then press [Alt] ⏎ to insert a line break.
   Type **Result** then press ⏎ to confirm.

3. To create the data series APRIL, MAY and JUNE in cells B4 to D4, click cell **B4** then type **APRIL**.
   Point to the fill handle on cell **B4** then drag it over cells **C4** and **D4**.

4. To create a custom data series containing the names SUMNER, FARELLI and CONROY, use the **Tools - Options** command then click the **Custom Lists** tab.
   Click the **NEW LIST** option in the **Custom lists** list box.
   In the **List entries** box, enter **SUMNER**, **FARELLI** and **CONROY** separating each name with ⏎.
   Click the **Add** button then click **OK**.

To insert the list in cells A5 to A7, click cell **A5**, type **SUMNER** then point to the fill handle and drag it over cells **A6** and **A7**.

5. To create a hyperlink to **3-1 Sales 1st Quarter** in cell **A15**, go to cell **A15** and use the **Insert - Hyperlink** command then if necessary, activate the **Existing File or Web Page** shortcut.
Click the **Current Folder** button then double-click the **3-1 Sales 1st Quarter** workbook in the **MOUS Excel 2002** folder.

To go to the **3-1 Sales 1st Quarter.xls** workbook, click the link when the pointer takes the shape of a hand.

6. To complete the Total by Salesperson worksheet in the 3-1 Sales 1st Quarter.xls workbook by inserting the sales figures made by Conroy in January, click the **Total by Salesperson** sheet tab.

Click cell **B7** and type **=**.

Click the **Conroy** sheet tab, click cell **B10** and confirm by pressing ⏎.

MANAGING DATA
Lesson 3.2: Finding and editing data

1 ▪ Modifying cell contents 78

2 ▪ Clearing cell contents and/or formatting 78

3 ▪ Finding a cell with a particular content 79

4 ▪ Finding a cell by its formatting 81

5 ▪ Finding files, items or Web pages 82

6 ▪ Replacing cell contents and/or formats 86

7 ▪ Checking the spelling of a text 88

Practice Exercise 3.2 91

🖥1 ▪ **Modifying cell contents**

▪ Double-click the cell you wish to modify:

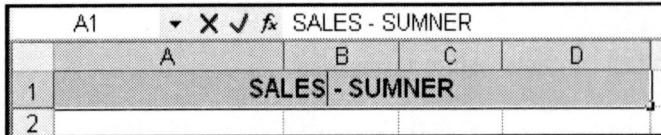

A1	▾ X ✓ ƒx SALES - SUMNER		
A	B	C	D
1	SALES - SUMNER		
2			

An insertion point (the flashing vertical bar) appears in the cell and Excel displays **Edit** *on the status bar.*

▪ Make your changes.

The new characters entered are added to the existing characters, providing Insert mode is active. If Overtype mode is active, the new characters replace the existing ones.

▪ To go from Insert to Overtype mode, and vice versa, press the ⌨Inser key.

▪ Confirm your changes by pressing the ⏎ key.

📄 *You can also click the cell then make your modifications directly in the formula bar.*

🖥2 ▪ **Clearing cell contents and/or formatting**

▪ Select the cells you want to clear then press the ⌨Del key to clear the contents.

This action deletes the cell contents but not the formatting.

▪ To remove the content and/or the formatting and/or the comments the cell contains, use the **Edit - Clear** command.

Edit		
↶	Undo Typing 'SALES FIGURES FOR SUMNER' in A1:D1	Ctrl+Z
↻	Repeat Close	Ctrl+Y
✂	Cut	Ctrl+X
📋	Copy	Ctrl+C
📋	Office Clipboard...	
📋	Paste	Ctrl+V
	Paste Special...	
	Paste as Hyperlink	
	Fill	▶
	Clear	▶
	Delete...	
	Delete Sheet	
	Move or Copy Sheet...	
🔍	Find...	Ctrl+F
	Replace...	Ctrl+H
	Go To...	Ctrl+G
	Links...	
	Object	

Clear submenu:

All	
Formats	
Contents	Del
Comments	

▪ Click the option that corresponds to the type of element you want to clear.

📄 *You can also select the cells you want to clear then drag the fill handle back over the selection.*

3 ▪ Finding a cell with a particular content

▪ If you want to search to the whole sheet, activate any cell. To search a particular part of the worksheet, select the corresponding range of cells.

▪ **Edit - Find** or Ctrl **F**

▪ Enter what you are looking for in the **Find what** text box.

- If you want to search just for the text entered, without taking into account any formatting, make sure that the text **No Format Set** appears to the right of the **Find what** text box. If this is not the case, open the drop-down list that appears on the **Format** button and choose **Clear Find Format**.

- If required, click the **Options** button to define how the search should be carried out:

Within	in the list, choose whether to search the current **Sheet** or all the sheets in the **Workbook**.
Search	in the list, choose in which direction the search should be carried out.
Look in	choose whether Excel should search for the item in the cell **Formulas**, the **Values** or the **Comments**.
Match case	tick this option if you want Excel to distinguish between upper and lower case characters in the search.
Match entire cell contents	tick this option if you want Excel to search for cells containing the whole search text, and only that text.

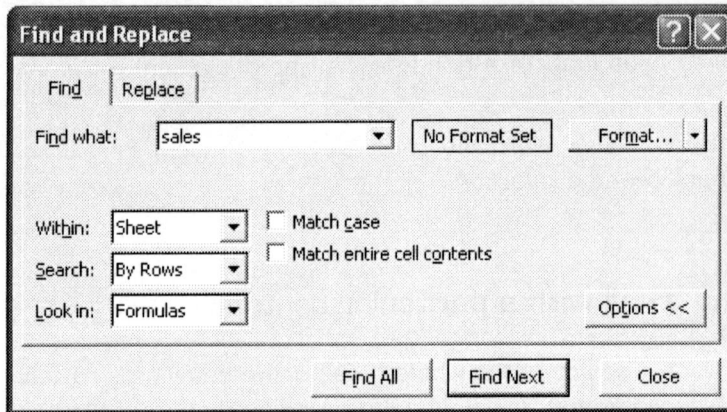

- To search cell by cell, click the **Find Next** button. If the cell found contains what you were looking for, click the **Close** button; if not, click **Find Next** to keep searching.

⁂ To search all cells simultaneously, click the **Find All** button. When you do this, a detailed list of the cells found appears in the bottom part of the dialog box.

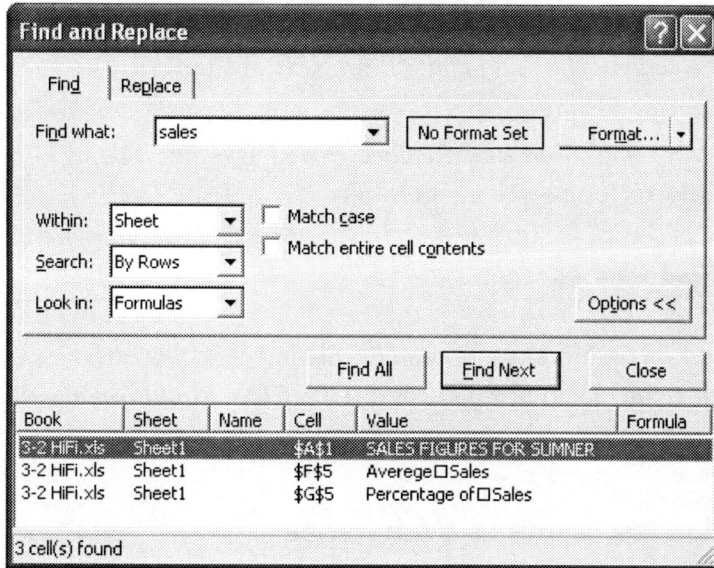

```
┌─────────────────────────────────────────────────────────────────┐
│ Find and Replace                                        [?][X]    │
│                                                                   │
│   Find │ Replace │                                                │
│                                                                   │
│  Find what: │sales              │ ▼ │ No Format Set │ Format... │▼│
│                                                                   │
│  Within:  │Sheet     │▼│   ☐ Match case                          │
│  Search:  │By Rows   │▼│   ☐ Match entire cell contents          │
│  Look in: │Formulas  │▼│                        Options <<        │
│                                                                   │
│                        │ Find All │  │ Find Next │  │ Close │     │
│                                                                   │
│  Book        Sheet    Name   Cell   Value                 Formula │
│  3-2 HiFi.xls Sheet1         $A$1   SALES FIGURES FOR SUMNER      │
│  3-2 HiFi.xls Sheet1         $F$5   Averege☐Sales                 │
│  3-2 HiFi.xls Sheet1         $G$5   Percentage of☐Sales           │
│  3 cell(s) found                                                  │
└─────────────────────────────────────────────────────────────────┘
```

⁂ Click one of the values in the list to select the corresponding cell. Click the **Close** button.

🔍 *When the **Find and Replace** dialog box is closed, you can continue the last search started by pressing* `Shift` `F4`.

4 ▪ Finding a cell by its formatting

⁂ Activate a single cell or select the part of the sheet in which you want to search.

⁂ **Edit - Find** or `Ctrl` **F**

⁂ If necessary, click the **Options** button to show the full range of search options.

⁂ Delete anything that may be still in the **Find what** box.

■ Click the **Format** button and in the **Find Format** dialog box, select the options for the required format.

The ***Choose Format From Cell*** *button allows you to select a cell and automatically retrieve all that cell's formatting attributes.*

■ Start the search, choosing either **Find Next** or **Find All**.

*When the **Find and Replace** dialog box has been closed, you can continue the last search made by pressing* Shift F4.

*You can search for both text and formatting simultaneously: enter the text in the **Find what** box then click the **Format** button to define the formatting options.*

*To cancel any formatting search criteria, click the arrow on the **Format** button in the dialog box and choose the **Clear Find Format** option.*

5 ▪ Finding files, items or Web pages

Carrying out a basic search

You can search for the names of files or items or for specific text within them. From Excel 2002 you can search for Office files (made in Excel, Word, PowerPoint or Access), Outlook items or Web pages.

■ Click the ▣ tool button on the **Standard** toolbar to open directly the **Basic Search** task pane.

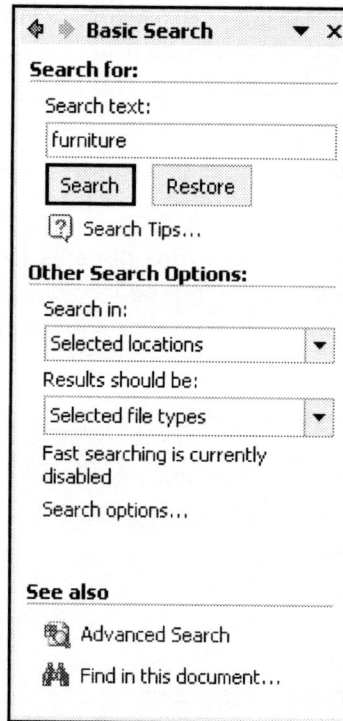

```
┌──────────────────────────────────────┐
│ ◆ ➤  Basic Search      ▼  ✕          │
│ Search for:                           │
│   Search text:                        │
│   ┌────────────────────────────────┐  │
│   │ furniture                      │  │
│   └────────────────────────────────┘  │
│   ┌──────────┐  ┌──────────┐          │
│   │  Search  │  │ Restore  │          │
│   └──────────┘  └──────────┘          │
│   [?] Search Tips...                  │
│                                       │
│   Other Search Options:               │
│   Search in:                          │
│   ┌──────────────────────────┐ ┌──┐   │
│   │ Selected locations       │ │▼ │   │
│   └──────────────────────────┘ └──┘   │
│   Results should be:                  │
│   ┌──────────────────────────┐ ┌──┐   │
│   │ Selected file types      │ │▼ │   │
│   └──────────────────────────┘ └──┘   │
│   Fast searching is currently         │
│   disabled                            │
│   Search options...                   │
│                                       │
│                                       │
│   See also                            │
│      ▓ Advanced Search                │
│      ♠ Find in this document...       │
└──────────────────────────────────────┘
```

* In the **Search text** box, enter the required text.

* To specify where the search should be carried out, use the options in the **Search in** drop-down list or give the complete file path for the search location.

* Expand the **Results should be** list and specify the type of files sought by activating (or deactivating) the types of items you want to include (or exclude).

* Click the **Search** button to start the search.

   *You may see a message telling you that the corresponding component is not installed. If this happens, insert the installation CD-ROM and click **Yes** to install the component.*

*If you wish to interrupt the search in progress, click the **Stop** button at the bottom of the task pane. If you stop a search or the search is complete, the **Modify** button appears instead. This **Modify** button returns the **Basic Search** task pane to the screen.*

- To open one of the items found (a file, Web page or Outlook item), click its name.

- When you point to an item, an arrow appears to the right of it. If you click the arrow, you open a list containing options so you can open the item in its application, create a new item from that one, copy the link into the clipboard or show its properties.

- When you have finished all your searches, you can close the task pane by clicking its ☒ button or deactivating the 🔍 tool.

*The options within the **Basic Search** task pane can also be found under the **Basic** tab in the **Search** dialog box (**File - Open**, open the **Tools** list and click the **Search** option).*

Carrying out an advanced search

- Click the 🔍 tool button on the **Standard** toolbar then click the **Advanced Search** link at the bottom of the task pane.

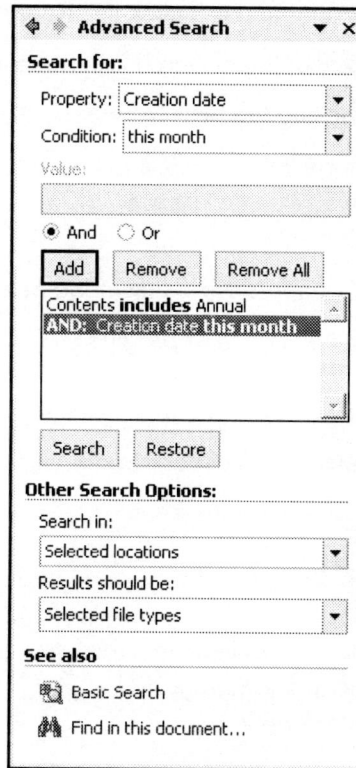

* To set each search criterion:

 - open the **Property** list and select the characteristic you want to include in the search,

 - set the search **Condition** in the corresponding box,

 - if required, enter a comparative value in the **Value** box,

 - click the **Add** button once you have finished defining your criterion.

 - if you wish to set another condition, select an operator: **And** if all the conditions must be met simultaneously or **If** if one or the other can be met,

 - if necessary, use the **Search in** list to define where the search should be carried out and indicate the type of items sought in the **Results should be** list.

* To remove a selected criterion, click the **Remove** button.

- To remove all the criteria in the list, click the **Remove All** button.

- To display the previously defined search criteria, click the **Restore** button.

- Start your search by clicking the **Search** button.

  You may see a message telling you that the corresponding component is not installed. If this happens, insert the Excel 2002 or Office XP CD-ROM and click ***Yes*** *to install the component.*

  The list of items found appears gradually in the ***Search Results*** *task pane.*

  If you wish to interrupt the search in progress, click the ***Stop*** *button at the bottom of the task pane. If you stop a search or the search is complete, the* ***Modify*** *button appears instead.*

- To return to the **Advanced Search** task pane, click the **Modify** button.

- When you have finished all your searches, you can close the task pane by clicking its ☒ button or deactivating the 🔍 tool.

  *The options within the **Advanced Search** task pane can also be found under the **Advanced** tab in the **Search** dialog box (**File - Open**, open the **Tools** list and click the **Search** option).*

6 ▪ Replacing cell contents and/or formats

It is possible to replace the text and/or format contained in several cells by another text and/or format. This technique also allows you to change text within formulas.

Replacing text

- If the replacement is to be carried out over the active worksheet or all the worksheets in the workbook, activate a single cell. To make the replacement in a portion of the active sheet, select the range of cells concerned.

- **Edit - Replace** or Ctrl **H**

- In the **Find what** box, enter the text you wish to replace.

You can enter letters, numbers, punctuation marks or wildcard characters (? which replaces one character and * which replaces several).

* In the **Replace with** box, enter the replacement text.

* As when searching cells, (cf. Finding a cell with a particular content) you can click the **Options** button and specify how and where Excel should look for the text you are replacing.

* To make the replacements one by one, click **Find Next** to go to the first cell containing the required text then click the **Replace** button (if you want to replace that value) or the **Find Next** button (to ignore that text and continue searching).

* To make all the replacements with a single action, click the **Replace All** button.

* Click the **Close** button when you have finished.

Replacing formatting

* Activate a cell or select the specific range of cells involved.

* **Edit - Replace** or Ctrl **H**

* If necessary, click the **Options** button to show all the search options.

* Delete any text that may still appear in the **Find what** or **Replace with** boxes.

* Click the first **Format** button and in the **Find Format** dialog box, select the required format options.

  The Choose Format From Cell button is used to select a cell and retrieve that cell's formatting automatically.

* Click **OK**.

* Click the second **Format** button and in the **Find Format** dialog box, select the required format options and click **OK**.

* Make your replacements one by one using the **Find Next** and **Replace** buttons or use the **Replace All** button to make all the replacements with a single action.

* Click the **Close** button.

📄 *You can replace text and formatting simultaneously. To do this, enter the text in the **Find what** and **Replace with** boxes and choose the formatting options by clicking the **Format** buttons.*

7 ▪ Checking the spelling of a text

▪ To check the spelling over a whole worksheet, activate any cell. To check a range of cells containing text, select those cells.

▪ **Tools - Spelling** or [ABC] or [F7]

Spelling: English (U.S.)

Not in Dictionary:
Averege

Suggestions:
Average

Dictionary language: English (U.S.)

Ignore Once | Ignore All | Add to Dictionary | Change | Change All | AutoCorrect | Options... | Undo Last | Cancel

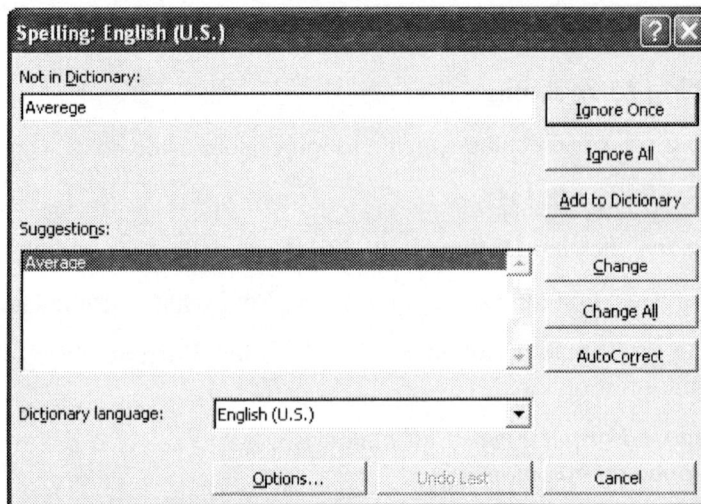

Excel examines the text and stops when it reaches an unknown word. A word is unknown if it is:

- *not included in the dictionary used by Excel,*

- *entered with an unusual combination of upper and lower case letters (for example, SAles),*

- *repeated (for example, that that one is…).*

This check is made from the main dictionary (from Excel) and as many custom dictionaries as you like (by default, the only existing one is CUSTOM.DIC).

» If the word is correctly spelt, click:

Ignore Once   to leave the word unchanged and continue checking.

Ignore All   to ignore the word here and every time it occurs subsequently.

Add to Dictionary to add the word to the active dictionary.

» If the word is incorrect, you can correct it by selecting one of the suggestions or by entering the correct text in the **Not in Dictionary** text box and clicking:

Change   to replace the incorrect word with the text you entered.

Change All   to replace the word here, and every time it occurs, with the entered text.

» You can also change this occurrence of the word by double-clicking one of the suggestions.

» In the case of a mistakenly repeated word, click the **Delete** button to remove it.

» When Excel has finished checking, the following dialog box appears:

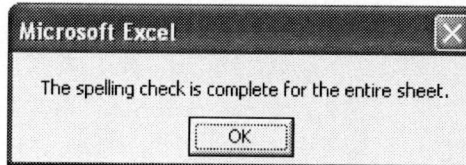

Microsoft Excel

The spelling check is complete for the entire sheet.

OK

» Click **OK**.

To create a custom dictionary, click the **Options** button on the **Spelling** dialog box then type the name of the new dictionary in the **Add words to** box then enter.

Custom dictionaries are stored by default in the following folders:

- In Windows 2000 and later: C:\Program Files\Common Files\Microsoft Shared\Proof folder.

- In Windows Millennium or Windows 98: C:\Windows_folder\Application Data\Microsoft\Proof folder or C:\Windows_folder\Profiles\User_name\ Application Data\Microsoft\Proof folder.

- In Windows NT 4.0: C:\Windows_folder\Profiles\User_name\Application Data\Microsoft\Proof folder.

Below, you can see **Practice Exercise** 3.2. This exercise is made up of 7 steps. If you do not know how to do one of the steps, go back to the title that corresponds to that particular lesson. When you have finished, you can check your work by reading the **Solution** that follows.

Steps that are likely to be tested during the MOUS exam are marked with this symbol: ▦. However, it is a good idea to complete the whole exercise to ensure you have understood everything covered in the lesson.

👉 Practice Exercise 3.2

To work on exercise 3.2, you should open the *3-2 HiFi.xls* workbook in the *MOUS Excel 2002* folder then activate *Sheet1* if necessary.

▦ 1. Change the text in cell **A1** to **SALES FIGURES FOR SUMNER**.

▦ 2. Clear the contents of cells **A20** to **D21** and just the format of cells **E6** to **E17**.

3. Look for the cells containing a value of **1000**, then close the **Find and Replace** dialog box.

4. Look for all the cells to which a **bold** format has been applied.

5. Using the task pane, look for all the workbooks in the **MOUS Excel 2002** folder containing the word **furniture**.

▦ 6. In cells **F5** and **G5**, replace the word **Sales** by the word **Turnover** and apply a **Red** colour to all the cells whose characters are in **bold** type.

7. Check the spelling of all the texts on **Sheet1** and make any necessary changes.

If you want to put what you have learnt into practice on a real document, you can work on summary exercise 3 for the MANAGING DATA section, that you can find at the end of this book.

It is often possible to perform a task in several different ways, but here, only the easiest solution is presented. You can go back to the corresponding lesson if you want to see other techniques you could use.

Solution to Exercise 3.2

1. To change the text in A1 to SALES FIGURES FOR SUMNER, double-click cell **A1**.
   Place the insertion point before the hyphen and press the [Del] key.
   Enter **FIGURES FOR** then confirm by pressing ⏎.

2. To clear the contents of cells A20 to D21, select cells **A20** to **D21** then press [Del].

   To clear the format of cells E6 to E17, select cells **E6** to **E17**, open the **Edit** menu then point to the **Clear** option.
   Click the **Formats** option.

3. To look for the cells containing the value 1000, click in cell **A1** then use the **Edit - Find** command.
   Enter **1000** in the **Find what** text box then activate the **Match entire cell contents** option (click **Options** if this option is hidden).
   Make sure the preview box between the **Find what** text box and the **Format** button contains the text **No Format Set**. If not, open the list on the **Format** button and choose the **Clear Find Format** option
   Click the **Find Next** button to start the search and see the first cell found.
   Click the **Find Next** button several times to see the other cells containing the value **1000**.
   When the search is finished, click the **Close** button to close the **Find and Replace** dialog box.

4. To find all the cells to which a bold format has been applied, activate cell **A1** and use the **Edit - Find** command.
If necessary, use the ⌐Del⌐ key to delete any contents remaining in the **Find what** box. If necessary, click the **Options** button to see the full list of search options.

Click the **Format** button, click the **Font** tab and choose **Bold** in the **Font style** list then click **OK**.
Click the **Find All** button to see a list of the 14 cells found during the search in the lower part of the **Find and Replace** dialog box.
Click the **Close** button.

5. To use the task pane to look for all the workbooks in the MOUS Excel 2002 folder containing the word «furniture», click the [ ] tool button to open the **Basic Search** task pane.
Enter **furniture** in the **Search text** text box.
Open the **Search in** list and deactivate all the options except the one referring to the MOUS Excel 2002 folder. To close this list, click a blank space on the task pane.
Open the **Results should be** list and deactivate all the options except the **Excel Files** option (under **Office Files**). To close this list, click a blank space on the task pane.
Click the **Search** button: the **Search Results** pane should display 6 results.
To close the **Search Results** pane, click the [X] button.

6. To replace the text «Sales» in cells F5 and G5 with «Turnover», click cell **A1** then use the **Edit - Replace** command.
Type **Sales** in the **Find what** text box then **Turnover** in the **Replace with** text box.
If necessary, deactivate the **Match entire cell contents** option and the **Match case** option.
Click the **Find Next** button followed by the **Replace** button. Click the **Find Next** button then **Replace** again.

To apply the colour **Red** to all the cells with a **Bold** formatting style, start by clearing the contents of the **Find what** and **Replace with** text boxes. Click the **Format** button next to the **Find what** text box.

Activate the **Font** tab, click **Bold** under **Font style** (making sure no colour is selected) and confirm your search criterion with **OK**.
Next, click the **Format** button next to the **Replace with** text box, click the **Font** tab and choose **Red** in the **Color** drop-down list. Choose **Bold** as the **Font style** and click **OK**.
Click the **Replace All** button.

Excel tells you it has made 14 replacements: click **OK** then close the **Find and Replace** dialog box with the **Close** button.

7. To check the spelling of the text in Sheet1, click cell **A1** of **Sheet1** then use the **Tools - Spelling** command.
Click the **Ignore Once** button then **Change** twice.
Click the **OK** button when the spelling check is finished.

MANAGING DATA
Lesson 3.3: Copying and moving

1 ▪ Copying cell contents to adjacent cells 98

2 ▪ Copying/moving cells 99

3 ▪ Copying/moving multiple items 100

4 ▪ Copying contents, calculation results or formats 102

5 ▪ Copying and transposing data 103

6 ▪ Copying cells and establishing a link 103

Practice Exercise 3.3 105

1 ▪ Copying cell contents to adjacent cells

This is a useful technique for copying text or formulas rapidly into adjoining cells.

⬛ Click the cell whose contents are to be copied.

⬛ Point to the cell's fill handle:

AVERAGE	PROGRESSION
5236	-2%
	13%
	-13%

The fill handle is the small black square in the active cell's bottom right corner. Notice how, when you point to it, the pointer changes shape.

⬛ Hold down the mouse button and drag towards the destination cell for the copy.

The cells over which you drag appear with a hatched border.

⬛ When the last destination cell is reached, release the mouse button.

*As soon as you finish copying, the **Auto Fill Options** button* *appears to the bottom right of the copied range.*

AVERAGE	PROGRESSION	
5236	-2%	
4385	13%	
4905	-13%	

○ Copy Cells
○ Fill Formatting Only
○ Fill Without Formatting

⬛ Click the button to see the options you can use in relation to the copy; you can just **Copy Cells** as they are, **Fill Formatting Only** (copy just the format) or **Fill Without Formatting** (copy just the contents).

▦2 ▪ Copying/moving cells

These copying techniques are used to move or copy into non-adjacent cells.

First method

This technique is usually used when the copied cells and destination cells can both be viewed on the same screen.

▪ Select the cells you wish to move or copy.

▪ Point to one of the edges of the selected group.

	A	B	C	
1	SALES RESULTS PER VENDOR			
2				
3				
4		Rate of commission	10%	
5				
6				

The pointer takes the shape of a white arrow, attached to a four-headed arrow. Be careful not to point to the fill handle!

▪ If you are making a copy, hold down the `Ctrl` key and drag the cells towards their new destination.

If you wish to move the cells, drag them towards the first destination cell.

When you make a copy, a small plus sign (+) appears to the right of the pointer.

▪ Release the mouse button, then, if you have been using it, the `Ctrl` key.

The cell contents and formatting are moved or copied into the destination cells.

Second method

▪ Select the cells you want to move or copy.

▪ If you wish to copy the cells, use **Edit - Copy** or 📋 or `Ctrl` C

MANAGING DATA
Lesson 3.3: Copying and moving

* If you wish to move the cells, use **Edit - Cut** or ✂ or ⌈Ctrl⌉ **X**

  *The selected cells appear in a flashing border. They have been copied or moved into the Windows clipboard. The **Clipboard** task pane may also appear on the screen.*

* Activate the first destination cell for the moved/copied data.

  Even if you are moving/copying several cells, only <u>one</u> destination cell needs to be activated.

* **Edit - Paste** or 📋 or ⌈Ctrl⌉ **V**

  *When you paste copied data, the **Paste** button 📋 appears to the bottom right of the destination range. If you wish, click this button for further options relating to what can be pasted.*

  📄 *The selected cells are still in the clipboard and you can paste them into other positions if you wish.*

📖3 ▪ Copying/moving multiple items

* If the task pane is not displayed, show it with the **View - Task Pane** command. Click the 🔽 button at the top of the pane and choose the **Clipboard** option, or use the **Edit - Office Clipboard** command.

  *If the **Show Office Clipboard Automatically** option is active (find this by clicking the **Options** button at the bottom of the **Clipboard** task pane), the **Clipboard** task pane appears automatically once you have made two consecutive move or copy actions or once you have used ⌈Ctrl⌉ **C** twice.*

* Select the cells concerned then transfer them to the clipboard with the **Cut** or **Copy** commands. Carry out this action as many times as necessary.

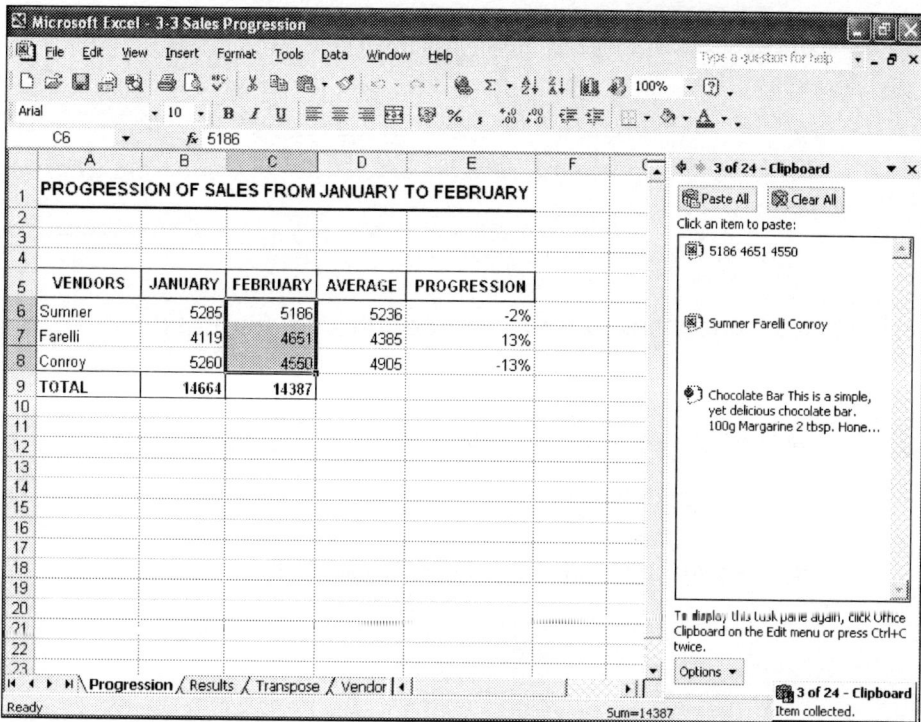

A preview of the cut and/or copied items appears in the **Clipboard** task pane. Up to 24 items can be stored there.

The **Clipboard** task pane contains elements copied or cut from various sources, including the Office applications (Excel, Word, PowerPoint, etc.).

* Activate the first destination cell.

* To paste one of the selected items from the **Clipboard** task pane, click its icon.

* Insert each item from the **Clipboard** task pane in this way, as many times as you like.

When you point to an item, an arrow appears on its right. Click this arrow to see options allowing you to **Paste** or **Delete** the item.

* If necessary, close the **Clipboard** task pane by clicking its ☒ button.

📄 *The* 📋 Paste All *button on the **Clipboard** task pane pastes in all the available items. They are copied in a column, one underneath the other. This button is not available if one of the elements is an image or object.*

*To empty the **Clipboard**, click the* 🗙 Clear All *button on the **Clipboard** task pane.*

4 ▪ Copying contents, calculation results or formats

* Select the cells you want to copy.

* Proceed as for an ordinary copy (**Edit - Copy**).

* Activate the first destination cell for the copy.

* Open the list attached to the 📋 ▾ tool button on the **Standard** toolbar:

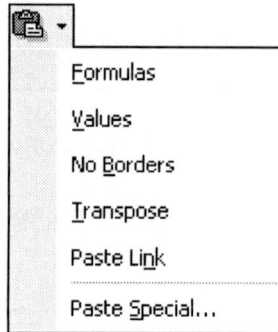

* Choose:

Formulas to copy the cell contents (formulas or values) without the associated formatting.

Values to copy just the results of formulas, again without formatting.

No Borders to copy the contents and the formats but not the borders.

Paste Special   to see further paste options, such as pasting formats, column widths, etc.

These options can also be found using the ***Edit - Paste Special*** command.

5 ▪ Copying and transposing data

This technique is used to transpose the columns and rows on a table when you copy it (the rows become columns and the columns become rows).

▪ Select the data you want to copy, start copying (**Edit - Copy**), then activate the first destination cell for the copy.

▪ Open the list on the [tool button icon] tool button and choose the **Transpose** option.

When you do this, the rows in the pasted data become columns and vice versa.

6 ▪ Copying cells and establishing a link

When a link is in place, any changes made to the data in the original Excel workbook are carried over into the file containing the exported data.

Copying Excel data into another application

▪ Open the Excel workbook containing the data you want to copy.

▪ **Edit - Copy** or [icon] or [Ctrl] **C**

▪ Open the other application (for example, Word) and the file into which you want to paste the Excel data.

▪ Click the place where the data should be pasted.

▪ **Edit - Paste Special** (in the target application)

▪ Activate the **Paste link** option.

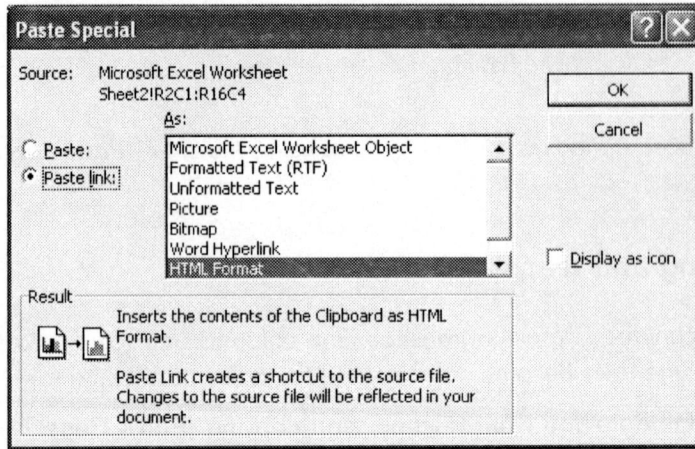

» From the **As** list, select the format in which you want to paste the data.

» Activate the **Display as icon** option if you want the linked data to be displayed in the form of an icon.

» Click **OK**.

Copying and linking data within an Excel sheet

» Select the data you wish to copy.

» Start the copying process (**Edit - Copy**).

» Activate the first target cell for the copied data.

» Expand the list on the [icon] tool button and choose the **Paste Link** option.

The destination cells now contain formulas that can show the contents of each source cell. If you modify a source value, it is carried over immediately into the target cell.

Creating a link as you copy does not automatically retrieve the cell formatting.

If you paste and create a link with an empty cell, Excel shows a zero value.

You can obtain the same result by inserting an =CELL type formula.

Below, you can see **Practice Exercise** 3.3. This exercise is made up of 6 steps. If you do not know how to do one of the steps, go back to the title that corresponds to that particular lesson. When you have finished, you can check your work by reading the **Solution** that follows.

Steps that are likely to be tested during the MOUS exam are marked with this symbol: ⊞. However, it is a good idea to complete the whole exercise to ensure you have understood everything covered in the lesson.

☞**Practice Exercise 3.3**

*To work on exercise 3.3, you should open the **3-3 Sales Progression.xls** workbook located in the **MOUS Excel 2002** folder.*

1. In the **Progression** worksheet, copy the contents of cell **D6** into the adjacent cells **D7** and **D8**.

⊞ 2. In the **Results** worksheet, move cells **B4** and **C4** towards cells **A4** and **B4**.

⊞ 3. Copy cells **A6** to **A8** and **C6** to **C8** on the **Progression** sheet then paste them into cells **A8** to **A10** and **B8** to **B10** on the **Results** sheet, using the Office Clipboard.

4. On the **Results** worksheet, copy the format of cell **D7** onto cells **B7** and **C7**.

5. Copy cells **A7** to **D11** on the **Results** sheet then paste them, transposing the data, onto the **Transpose** worksheet. The first destination cell for the copy should be cell **A3**.

6. Copy cells **A8** to **A10** on the **Results** worksheet onto cells **A5** to **A7** on the **Vendor Totals** sheet, establishing a link with the copy. Use the **Paste Options** button [icon] to make the link.

If you want to put what you have learnt into practice on a real document, you can work on summary exercise 3 for the MANAGING DATA section, that you can find at the end of this book.

It is often possible to perform a task in several different ways, but here, only the easiest solution is presented. You can go back to the corresponding lesson if you want to see other techniques you could use.

Solution to Exercise 3.3

1. To copy the contents of cell D6 into the adjacent cells D7 and D8 on the Progression sheet, click the **Progression** sheet tab, then click cell **D6**. Point to the fill handle on cell **D6**, then drag the fill handle down to cell **D8**.

2. To move cells B4 and C4 to cells A4 and B4 on the Results sheet, click the **Results** tab then select cells **B4** and **C4**.
   Point to one of the edges of the selected range then drag it to cell **A4**.

3. To copy cells A6 to A8 and C6 to C8 on the Progression sheet then paste them onto cells A8 to A10 and B8 to B10 on the Results sheet, start by displaying the **Clipboard** task pane with the **Edit - Office Clipboard** command.

   Click the **Progression** tab, select cells **A6** to **A8** and use **Edit - Copy**; select cells **C6** to **C8** and use **Edit - Copy** again.
   Click the **Results** tab.
   Click cell **A8** then click the **Sumner Farelli Conroy** item that you can see in the **Clipboard** task pane, to paste in that range of cells.
   Click cell **B8** then the **5186 4651 4550** item in the **Clipboard** task pane, to paste in that range of cells.

4. To copy the format of cell D7 onto cells B7 and C7 on the Results sheet, click the **Results** tab then cell **D7**.
Use **Edit - Copy** then select cells **B7** and **C7**.

Open the list attached to the tool button on the **Standard** toolbar. Activate the **Paste Special** option then choose **Formats** and confirm with **OK**.
Press Esc to deactivate the copying process.

5. To copy cells A7 to D11 on the Results worksheet and paste them, transposing the data, onto the Transpose sheet, click the **Results** sheet tab then select cells **A7** to **D11**.

Click the tool then the **Transpose** tab.

Click cell **A3** then open the list on the tool button and choose **Transpose**.

6. To copy cells A8 to A10 on the Results sheet to cells A5 to A7 on the Vendor Totals sheet, and establish a link between the cells, start by clicking the **Results** tab.

Select cells **A8** to **A10**, click the tool then the **Vendor Totals** tab.

Click cell **A5**, open the list on the button then click the **Paste Link** option.

MANAGING DATA
Lesson 3.4: Filters

1 ▪ Creating and using a simple filter 110

2 ▪ Filtering by several criteria 112

3 ▪ Showing all the records again 112

Practice Exercise 3.4 113

▣1 ▪ Creating and using a simple filter

A filter is used to select records that correspond to a set criterion.

Activating AutoFilter

▪ Activate one of the cells in the list of data.

▪ **Data - Filter - AutoFilter**

Each field becomes a drop-down list that can be opened by clicking the down arrow to the right of the field name.

Filtering by one of the values listed

▪ Open the list associated with the field concerned:

	B	C	D	E	F
	First Nam ▾	**Address** ▾	**PC/City** ▾	**Se** ▾	**Ag** ▾
	Carla	56 Lawrence St	4000 Westpc (All)		15
	John	37 Chambers St	4000 Westpc (Top 10...)		16
	Andrew	19 Playton Place	4000 Westpc F (Custom...)		19
	Brendan	32 Yarmouth Ave	4000 Westpc M		25
	Ken	8 Waterford Dr	4000 Westport	M	15
	Christine	56 Harvey St	4100 Tewesbury	F	13

Each list includes all the values in the field.

▪ Click the value that interests you.

Only the records that correspond to the filter value can now be seen on the screen, those that do not correspond are hidden. The row numbers of the records displayed change colour.

Filtering by a specific criterion

▪ Open the list associated with the required field.

▪ Choose the **(Custom...)** option.

▪ In the first list box, select an operator of comparison.

※ Activate the text box next to it and enter the compare value.

Custom AutoFilter

Show rows where:
Age

| is greater than or equal to ▼ | 21 ▼ |

● And ○ Or

| ▼ | ▼ |

Use ? to represent any single character
Use * to represent any series of characters

OK   Cancel

※ Click **OK**.

Filtering the highest and lowest values

※ Open the list associated with the field concerned.

※ Click the **(Top 10...)** option.

※ Indicate whether you want to see the **Top** values or the **Bottom** values.

※ Specify how many records containing the top/bottom values you want to see (for example, the 4 highest or the 10 lowest).

※ Choose **Items** to filter all the records corresponding to the criteria (top or bottom) or **Percent** to filter a number of rows corresponding to a percentage of the total number of values in the list.

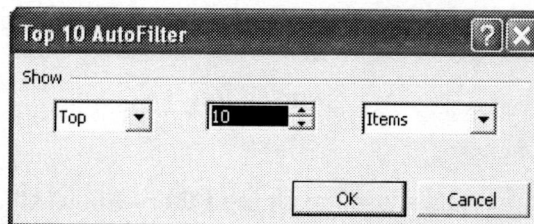

Top 10 AutoFilter

Show

| Top ▼ | 10 ▲▼ | Items ▼ |

OK   Cancel

■ Click **OK**.

📄 *To deactivate the AutoFilter, use **Data - Filter** and click the **AutoFilter** option again to turn off the feature.*

📖2 ▪ Filtering by several criteria

Two criteria for the same field

■ Activate the **AutoFilter** (cf. Creating and using a simple filter).

■ Open the list for the field concerned.

■ Click the **(Custom...)** option.

■ Define the first filter criterion.

■ Indicate how the two criteria are to be combined:

- if both must be satisfied together, choose **And**,

- if either one or the other must be satisfied, choose **Or**.

■ Enter your second condition.

■ Click **OK**.

Criteria concerning several fields, combined with "and"

■ Activate **AutoFilter**.

■ Set the conditions in each field concerned.

📖3 ▪ Showing all the records again

■ If only one filter is active, open the drop-down list on the field that is filtered and click the **All** option.

■ If several filters are active, use the **Data - Filter - Show All** command.

Below, you can see **Practice Exercise** 3.4. This exercise is made up of 3 steps. If you do not know how to do one of the steps, go back to the title that corresponds to that particular lesson. When you have finished, you can check your work by reading the **Solution** that follows.

All the steps in this exercise are likely to be tested in the MOUS exam.

☞ Practice Exercise 3.4

*To work on exercise 3.4, open the **3-4 Sport Base.xls** workbook, located in the **MOUS Excel 2002** folder, then if necessary, activate the **Base** worksheet.*

1. Using a simple filter, display on the screen only the list of female club members.

2. Display on the screen only female club members aged between 15 and 22, inclusive.

3. Show all the records in the list in 3-4 Sport Base again then deactivate the AutoFilter.

If you want to put what you have learnt into practice on a real document, you can work on summary exercise 3 for the MANAGING DATA section, that you can find at the end of this book.

It is often possible to perform a task in several different ways, but here, only the easiest solution is presented. You can go back to the corresponding lesson if you want to see other techniques you could use.

Solution to Exercise 3.4

1. To use a simple filter to display on the screen only the list of female club members, activate the **AutoFilter** using the **Data - Filter - AutoFilter** command. Open the list on the **Sex** field and activate the **F** option.

2. To display on the screen only female club members aged between 15 and 22, inclusive, keep the filter applied to the **Sex** field in the last step, then open the list on the **Age** field, click the **(Custom...)** option and give two custom criteria as shown below:

Click **OK** to confirm these criteria.

3. To show all the records in the list in 3-4 Sport Base again, use the **Data - Filter - Show All** command.

   To deactivate the AutoFilter, use the **Data - Filter - AutoFilter** command.

MANAGING DATA
Lesson 3.5: Sharing data through a Web site

1 ▪ Basic principles and configuration 116

▣ 2 ▪ Managing discussion comments from Excel 2002 122

❚ Practice Exercise 3.5 127

1 ▪ Basic principles and configuration

Overview

When working with others, you may find it useful to share documents with other members of your team and to attach comments to shared workbooks. To do this, you need to save the workbook on a team Web site based on SharePoint Team services, stored on a discussion server. The team Web site is a place on the Internet, installed and configured by your network administrator, where you and your colleagues can communicate, share documents and collaborate on common projects.

A simple Web browser, such as Internet Explorer, can access the team Web site so you can participate in various discussions on a particular workbook or subject, or answer questions currently being asked. SharePoint Web sites have many different features for a variety of purposes, but this book will deal only with how to manage comments in discussions concerning shared workbooks and working with such comments in Excel.

Although you can «converse» with colleagues on the team Web site using a browser such as Internet Explorer, you can also use the Microsoft Office XP applications (Excel, Word, PowerPoint etc.) to work directly with the site, using an integrated feature called Web Discussions. You can use this feature to manage discussion comments (enter, edit, delete, etc.) directly in the Office XP application. Updating the saved files is handled discreetly by the discussion server.

Adding or modifying a link to a discussion server

▪ Create or open a workbook.

▪ **Tools - Online Collaboration - Web Discussions**

The **Web Discussions** toolbar appears at the bottom of the screen:

If no link to the discussion server has been defined, this screen may appear:

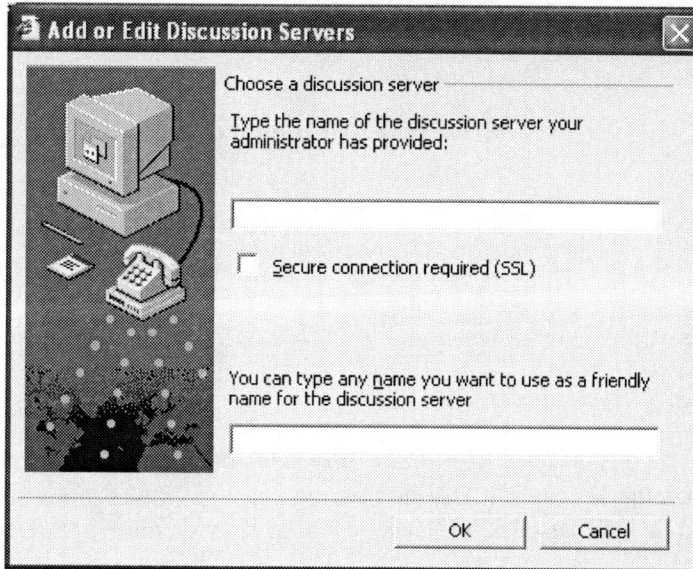

If this is the case, you can skip the next two points and go directly to entering the name of the server.

* Click the **Discussions** button then **Discussion Options**.

* To create a new link to a discussion server, click the **Add** button in the **Discussion Options** dialog box.

* Enter the name (or IP address) of the discussion server with which you want to exchange comments.

* If you wish **You can type any name you want to use as a friendly name for the discussion server**. Click the corresponding text box and enter the required name.

Choose a discussion server

Type the name of the discussion server your administrator has provided:

http://10.0.0.140

☐ Secure connection required (SSL)

You can type any name you want to use as a friendly name for the discussion server

My Team

* Click **OK**.

* To change the address or name of the selected discussion server, click the **Edit** button on the **Discussion Options** dialog box then make the required changes in the **Add or Edit Discussion Servers** dialog box. Confirm with **OK**.

Discussion Options ☒

Select a discussion server:

My Team (http://10.0.0.140/) ▼

Add... | Edit... | Remove

Discussion fields to display:

☑ Display name ☑ User name ☑ Subject
☑ Text ☑ Time

☑ Show closed discussions

OK | Cancel

* To delete the link to a discussion server, select it in the **Select a discussion server** list and click the **Remove** button. Click **OK** to confirm deleting the link.

- If you want the **Display name** or **User name** (network identifier) of a comment's author to appear in the **Discussion** pane, tick the appropriate option(s) in the **Discussion fields to display** frame.

- If you want the discussion **Subject**, the **Time** a comment was saved and a comment's **Text** to appear in the **Discussion** pane, tick the appropriate option(s) in the **Discussion fields to display** frame.

- To **Show closed discussions**, tick the corresponding option.

  The settings you choose for discussion fields and the display of closed discussions always apply, no matter which discussion server is selected.

- Click **OK** to confirm your settings.

- To close the **Web Discussions** toolbar, click its **Close** button.

Creating a shortcut to a team Web site

The shared documents that you intend to discuss with other authorised users are stored on the discussion server. To save or open these documents quickly and easily, you should create a shortcut (or network place) to the server.

- If necessary, open the task pane with the **View - Task Pane** command, then open the list ▼ at the top of the task pane and click the **New Workbook** option.

- If you are using Windows XP, 2000 or Windows Me, click the **Add Network Place** link at the bottom of the task pane. Activate the **Create a shortcut to an existing Network Place** option in the **Add Network Place Wizard** window.

  If you are using Windows 98 or NT 4.0, click the **Add Web Folder** link at the bottom of the task pane. Activate the **Create a shortcut to an existing Web Folder** option.

- Click the **Next** button.

- In the **Location** box, enter the URL address of the team Web server supplied by your network administrator; this is the server that the shortcut will access.

- Click the **Shortcut name** box and if required, change the suggested name.

By default, Excel suggests that you use the server's name for the shortcut.

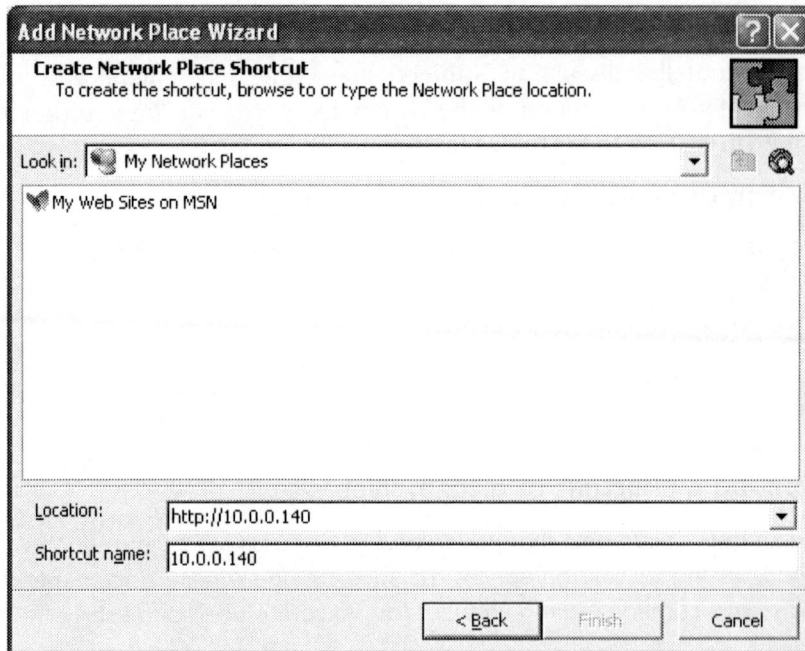

Add Network Place Wizard ? X

Create Network Place Shortcut
To create the shortcut, browse to or type the Network Place location.

Look in: My Network Places

My Web Sites on MSN

Location: http://10.0.0.140

Shortcut name: 10.0.0.140

< Back | Finish | Cancel

* Click the **Finish** button.

Creating a shared document for a team

If you want each user on the team Web site to be able to work on a shared document, you must save the document in a document library on the discussion server (a SharePoint Team Services team Web site).

* Create or open the workbook that you want to share with your team.

* **File - Save As**

* In the **Save As** dialog box, click the **My Network Places** button (Windows XP, 2000 or Me) or the **Web Folders** button (Windows 98 or NT 4.0), on the **Places Bar**.

* Click the network shortcut that leads to your team Web site.

* If you are prompted to identify yourself, enter your **User name** and **Password** and confirm with **OK**.

The name(s) of the document library (or libraries) available on the site appear(s).

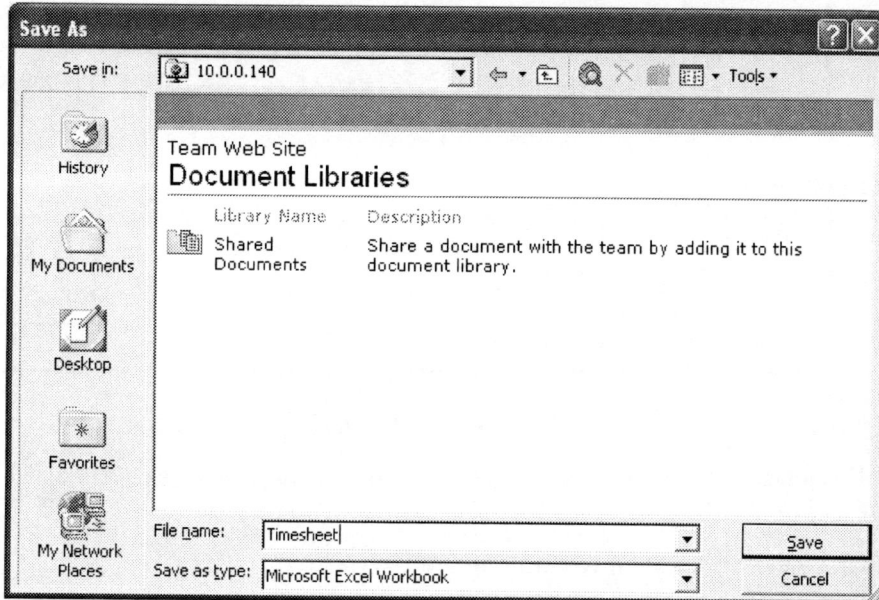

By default, a **Shared Documents** library is available. However, other libraries may have been created by the administrator or other users with the appropriate permissions, using the features in Microsoft SharePoint.

* Double-click the name of the library in which you want to save the workbook.

The contents of the document library appear on the screen.

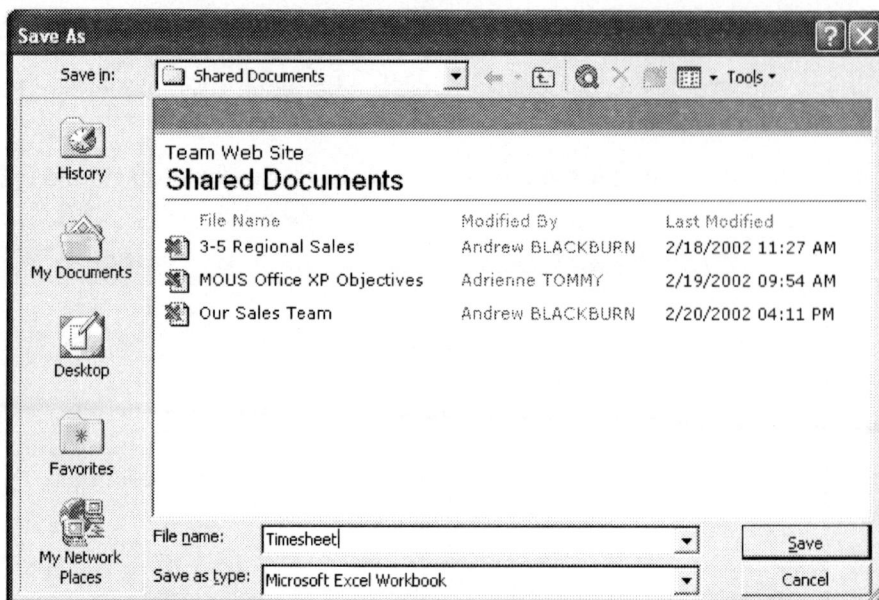

- If necessary, modify the **File name** before clicking the **Save** button.

  This saves the workbook on the team Web site; the workbook stays active in your Excel application.

- Close the workbook if you do not need to make any other changes to it.

📄 *If the shared workbook is currently being used, other team users will be able to open it only in <u>read-only</u> mode.*

🪟2 ▪ **Managing discussion comments from Excel 2002**

Opening a shared document

- To open a shared workbook, use the **File - Open** command then click **My Network Places** or **Web Folders** (depending on your version of Windows).

- Double-click the network shortcut for the team Web site on which the shared document is located.

- Double-click the name of the document library containing the required workbook.

- Double-click the name of the workbook you wish to open.

- Use the **Tools - Online Collaboration - Web Discussions** command to display the **Web Discussions** toolbar.

Creating, modifying or deleting a discussion comment

- Open the shared document and display the **Web Discussions** toolbar.

- To create a new discussion topic, click the **Discussions** button on the **Web Discussions** toolbar then click the **Insert about the Workbook** option (or click the ⬚ tool button).

- Enter the **Discussion subject** then type your message in the **Discussion text** box.

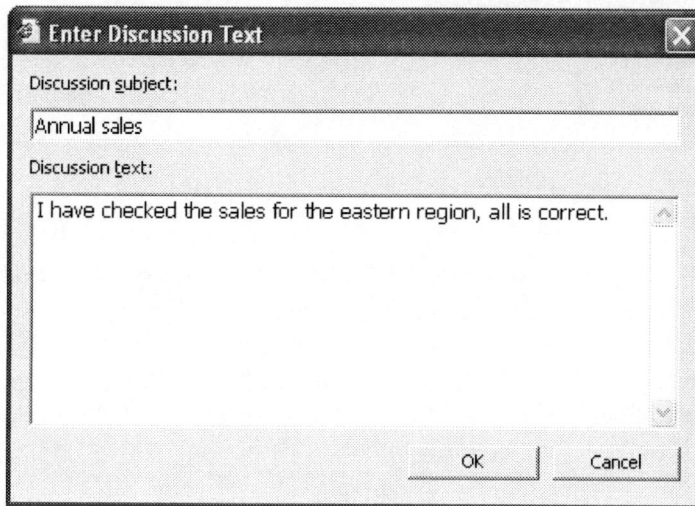

- Click **OK** to confirm your comment.

The comment you entered can be seen in the **Discussion** pane, between the worksheet and the **Web Discussions** toolbar.

The fields displayed depend on the defined **Discussion Options** (**Discussions** button).

* To change the comment text, click the ⬚▾ tool button to open the shortcut menu associated with the comment then click the **Edit** option. Make your required changes then confirm with the **OK** button.

* To delete the comment, click the ⬚▾ tool button then click the **Delete** option. Click **Yes** to confirm the deletion.

If the **Delete** option is greyed-out, this means you do not have the permissions required to delete the comment.

To show or hide the **Discussion** pane, click the [icon] tool button. Team members with **Contributor** or **Browser** permissions on the team Web site cannot modify shared documents.

To print comments, click the **Discussions** button on the **Web Discussions** toolbar and click the **Print Discussions** option.

Replying to a discussion comment

* Open the shared document and display the **Web Discussions** toolbar.

* To reply to a comment, click the [icon] tool button to open the shortcut menu associated with the comment and click the **Reply** option.

The **Enter Discussion Text** dialog box opens, using the same **Discussion subject**.

* Enter your reply in the **Discussion text** box and confirm with **OK**.

A message reply appears in the **Discussion** pane under the original message, slightly indented towards the right.

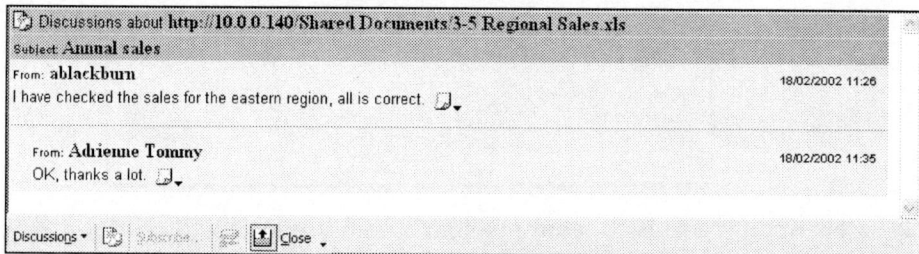

By default, messages appear in the **Discussion** pane classified by **Subject**.

Closing a discussion or reopening a closed discussion

* Open the shared document and display the **Web Discussions** toolbar.

* To close a discussion, click the [icon] tool button on the first message in the discussion then click the **Close Item and Replies** option.

The first message and its replies appear greyed-out: no new message can be added to this conversation unless you reactivate it.

■ To close only a comment, click the ⬚▾ tool button associated with the message and click the **Close** option.

The comment appears greyed-out: no new replies can be added, unless you reactivate the comment.

■ To reactivate a closed discussion or comment, click the ⬚▾ tool button associated with it and choose the **Activate** option.

Filtering discussion comments

■ Open the shared document and display the **Web Discussions** toolbar.

■ Click the **Discussions** button on the **Web Discussions** toolbar then choose the **Filter Discussions** option.

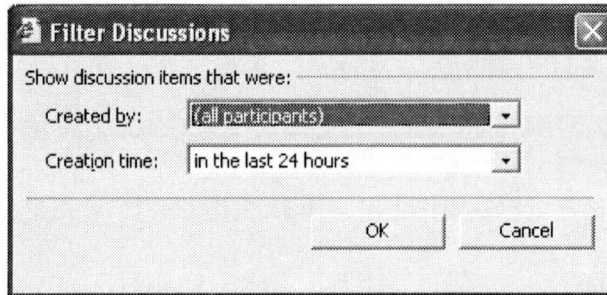

■ To filter comments by a team member's name, open the drop-down list on the **Created by** field and click the required name. If you do not want to filter by member names, make sure the **(all participants)** option is active.

■ To filter comments by **Creation time**, open the appropriate drop-down list and click the required filter.

■ Click **OK** to activate the filter(s) you have defined.

🔍 *To deactivate filters, click the **Filter Discussions** option in the list on the **Discussions** button and choose the **(all participants)** option in the **Created by** list and the **(anytime)** option in the **Creation time** list.*

Below, you can see **Practice Exercise** 3.5. This exercise is made up of 2 steps. If you do not know how to do one of the steps, go back to the title that corresponds to that particular lesson. When you have finished, you can check your work by reading the **Solution** that follows.

Steps that are likely to be tested during the MOUS exam are marked with this symbol: ▣. However, it is a good idea to complete the whole exercise to ensure you have understood everything covered in the lesson.

☞ **Practice Exercise 3.5**

To work on exercise 3.5, you need to:

- have access to a team Web site,

*- open the **3-5 Regional Sales.xls** workbook in the **MOUS Excel 2002** folder.*

1. Save the **3-5 Regional Sales.xls** workbook under the name of **Regions.xls**, in the **Shared Documents** library on the team Web site to which you have access. Close the workbook.

▣ 2. Open the **Regions.xls** workbook in the **Shared Documents** library on your team Web site, then make the following changes:

   - Create a new discussion subject called **Annual sales** and enter this text as the message: **Could everyone add any comments or corrections before the meeting? Thank you.**
   Confirm your entry.

   - Replace the word **any** in the discussion text by the text **his/her**.

If you want to put what you have learnt into practice on a real document, you can work on summary exercise 3 for the MANAGING DATA section, that you can find at the end of this book.

MANAGING DATA
Exercise 3.5: Sharing data through a Web site

It is often possible to perform a task in several different ways, but here, only the easiest solution is presented. You can go back to the corresponding lesson if you want to see other techniques you could use.

Solution to Exercise 3.5

1. To save the workbook under the name of Regions.xls in the Shared Documents library on the team Web site to which you have access, use the **File - Save As** command.

   Click the **My Network Places** button (on Windows 2000/Me/XP) or the **Web Folders** button (on Windows 98/NT4) on the **Places Bar** on the left of the **Save As** dialog box.

   Click the network shortcut that leads to the team Web site on which you work.

   If necessary, identify yourself with your user name and password. Double-click the **Shared Documents** library.

   Enter **Regions.xls** in the **File name** text box (in general, it is a good idea to avoid spaces in Web file names).

   Click the **Save** button.

   Use the **File - Close** command to close the **Regions.xls** workbook.

2. To open the Regions.xls workbook in the Shared Documents library on the team Web site to which you have access, use the **File - Open** command and click the **Web Folders** or **My Network Places** button (this depends on your version of Windows).

   Double-click the network shortcut that will take you to your team Web site then double-click the **Shared Documents** library.

   Double-click the **Regions.xls** workbook to open it.

   If necessary, display the **Web Discussions** toolbar using the **Tools - Online Collaboration - Web Discussions** command.

To create a new discussion subject called Annual sales, click the [icon] tool button and fill in the **Enter Discussion Text** dialog box, following the example below:

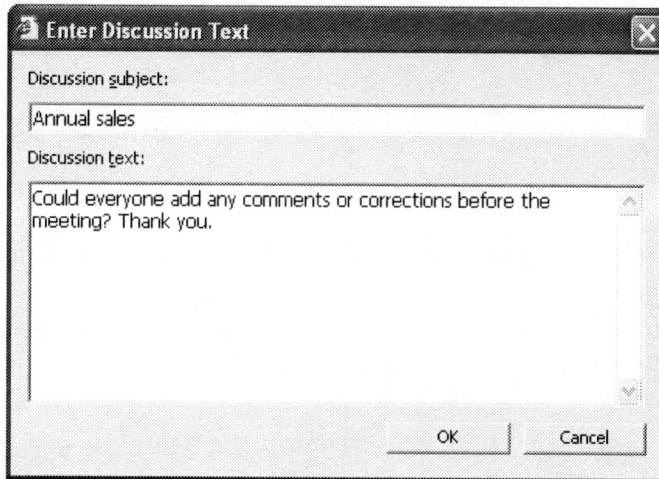

```
Enter Discussion Text                                        X

Discussion subject:
Annual sales
Discussion text:
Could everyone add any comments or corrections before the
meeting? Thank you.



                                        OK          Cancel
```

Click **OK** to confirm your text.

To replace the word «any» in the discussion text by the text «his/her», click the [icon] tool button on the message called **Annual Sales** then click the **Edit** option. Select the word **any** in the message by double-clicking the word then type **his/her** and confirm with **OK**.

Exercise 3.5: Sharing data through a Web site

CALCULATIONS
Lesson 4.1: Formulas

1 ▪ Entering calculation formulas 132

2 ▪ Modifying formulas 134

3 ▪ Using AutoSum to add cells 134

4 ▪ Including absolute cell references in a formula 136

Practice Exercise 4.1 138

CALCULATIONS
Lesson 4.1: Formulas

⊞1 ▪ Entering calculation formulas

- Activate the cell which will display the result.

- Type =

  *The word **Enter** appears on the status bar.*

- Activate the first cell involved in the calculation.

  *This cell is shown with a flashing border and its reference appears in the formula bar. The status bar now shows you are in **Point** mode.*

- Type in the mathematical operation to be carried out:

+	for addition
-	for subtraction
/	for division
*	for multiplication
%	for percentage
^	to raise to a power (exponentiation)

- Click the next cell involved in the calculation and enter the appropriate operator: continue building your formula in this way.

  If you like, you can enter a value instead of using the contents of a cell.

  While you are still building your formula, the cells that are involved in it are framed in coloured borders.

You can follow the development of the formula on the formula bar:

SUM	▾ X ✓ fx	=D5*E5		
	C	D	E	F	G
2					
3					
4	SALE PRICE	PROFIT MARGIN	QUANTITY	PROFIT MADE	SHARE OF PROFIT
5	258.75	51.75	25	=D5*E5	
6	538.80	89.80	18		

» If you are using several mathematical operators, you may need to add brackets to your formula to group the values linked by certain operators.

For example, =10/2*3 does not give the same result as =10/(2*3).

» When you reach the last cell, press the ⏎ key or click the ✔ button on the formula bar to confirm your formula.

The calculation result appears in the cell but the cell's true content is the formula, which is displayed in the formula bar when the cell is active.

📄 *A calculation formula can contain up to 1024 characters.*

> *Formulas in a table are recalculated automatically whenever you change the values involved in them. If this recalculation takes too long, you can stop automatic recalculation by activating one of these options: **Manual** or **Automatic except tables** (**Tools - Options - Calculation** tab). If you deactivate automatic recalculation, you can recalculate manually by pressing the F9 key.*

> *When you modify a calculation formula, the cell references that make it up appear in different colours on the formula bar. On the worksheet, each cell or cell range involved in the formula is bordered in the corresponding colour.*

> *The formula palette makes it easier to insert functions into your formulas (cf. Lesson 4.2 - Functions).*

> *To insert a formula in one sheet that refers to cells in another sheet, see Calculating values from different sheets in Lesson 3.1.*

CALCULATIONS
Lesson 4.1: Formulas

If you know the cell references, you can type them in rather than using the mouse or arrow keys to activate them.

Remember that a quick way of copying formulas from one cell into adjacent cells is to use the fill handle, in the bottom right corner of the active cell.

▪ Modifying formulas

※ Double-click the cell containing the formula you want to modify.

The cell references that make up the formula appear in different colours. In the worksheet, a border of the same colour surrounds each cell or cell range existing in the formula.

※ Edit the formula, deleting characters as required with the ⌷Del⌷ key and/or entering new characters directly in the cell or in the formula palette.

※ Press ⏎ to confirm your modifications.

▪ Using AutoSum to add cells

※ Activate the cell that will display the result.

※ Click the **AutoSum** tool button ⅀ or press ⌷Alt⌷ =.

SUM	▾	X ✓ ƒx	=SUM(F5:F19)		
	C	D	E	F	G
4	SALE PRICE	PROFIT MARGIN	QUANTITY	PROFIT MADE	SHARE OF PROFIT
5	258.75	51.75	25	1293.75	
6	538.80	89.80	18	1616.40	
7	238.80	39.80	42	1671.60	
8	518.70	119.70	58	6942.60	
9	58.50	13.50	57	769.50	
10	33.80	7.80	120	936.00	
11	183.30	42.30	14	592.20	
12	127.40	29.40	48	1411.20	
13	423.80	195.80	22	4307.60	
14	296.40	68.40	21	1436.40	
15	450.00	90.00	65	5850.00	
16	575.00	115.00	37	4255.00	
17	140.00	28.00	45	1260.00	
18	204.10	47.10	30	1413.00	
19	148.20	34.20	57	1949.40	
20				=SUM(F5:F19)	
21				SUM(**number1**, [number2], ...)	
22					

Excel displays the integrated function called SUM() and tries to guess which cells you want to add up (usually the group of cells above the formula).

- If you are not satisfied with this selection, use the mouse to change it.

- Confirm by pressing ⏎.

*When you select a range of cells containing numerical values, Excel displays the sum of these values in the status bar, by default. If you right-click this result on the status bar, you can choose another function so you can display the average, the number of non-blank cells (**Count**), the number of cells containing numerical values (**Count Nums**), the highest value (**Max**) or lowest value (**Min**) of the cells in the range.*

CALCULATIONS
Lesson 4.1: Formulas

4 ▪ Including absolute cell references in a formula

This technique is used to "fix" a cell reference and ensure it does not evolve when the formula is copied.

In the following example, the formula in cell G5 needs to be copied into cells G6 to G20. However, when you copy into cell G6, the formula will become =F6/F21...but cell F21 is empty! To obtain a correct result, the formula needs to be =F6/F20. You must make the reference of cell F20 absolute before copying the formula:

SUM ▾ X ✓ ƒₓ =F5/F20		
	E	F	G
4	QUANTITY	PROFIT MADE	SHARE OF PROFIT
5	25	1293.75	=F5/F20
6	18	1616.40	
7	42	1671.60	
8	58	6942.60	
9	57	769.50	
10	120	936.00	
11	14	592.20	
12	48	1411.20	
13	22	4307.60	
14	21	1436.40	
15	65	5850.00	
16	37	4255.00	
17	45	1260.00	
18	30	1413.00	
19	57	1949.40	
20		35704.65	
21			

▪ Start entering the formula and stop after the cell reference that you want to make absolute. If you are modifying an existing formula, click the reference of the cell concerned.

▪ Press F4.

The cell reference now contains $ signs before the column letter and before the row number:

SUM	▼ X ✓ *fx* =F5/$F$20	
E	**F**	**G**
QUANTITY (4)	**PROFIT MADE**	**SHARE OF PROFIT**
25 (5)	1293.75	=F5/$F$20
18 (6)	1616.40	
42 (7)	1671.60	
58 (8)	6942.60	
57 (9)	769.50	
120 (10)	936.00	
14 (11)	592.20	
48 (12)	1411.20	
22 (13)	4307.60	
21 (14)	1436.40	
65 (15)	5850.00	
37 (16)	4255.00	
45 (17)	1260.00	
30 (18)	1413.00	
57 (19)	1949.40	
(20)	35704.65	
(21)		

※ Complete the formula if necessary then enter.

🖰 *When you press* F4*, you obtain an absolute cell reference; press* F4 *again and only the row reference remains absolute; if you press* F4 *a third time, it is the column reference that is absolute.*

CALCULATIONS
Exercise 4.1: Formulas

Below, you can see **Practice Exercise** 4.1. This exercise is made up of 4 steps. If you do not know how to do one of the steps, go back to the title that corresponds to that particular lesson. When you have finished, you can check your work by reading the **Solution** that follows.

All the steps in this exercise are likely to be tested in the MOUS exam.

☞ Practice Exercise 4.1

*To work on exercise 4.1, you should open the **4-1 Furniture.xls** workbook in the **MOUS Excel 2002** folder then, if necessary, activate **Sheet1**.*

1. In cell **F5**, enter a formula that will multiply the **Profit Margin** by the **Quantity**. Next, copy the content of cell **F5** into the adjacent cells **F6** to **F19**.

2. In cell **D13**, the margin made by the product **Rectangular table** is wrong. The formula subtracts the Cost Price of the Wardrobe 2 door article from the Sale Price of the Rectangular table.
   You should modify the formula in cell **D13** so the Cost Price for the Rectangular table is subtracted from the Sale Price of the Rectangular table.

3. Find the total **Profit Made** and show the result in **F20**. Use the AutoSum function to do this.

4. In cell **G5**, calculate the share of profit made by the Sofa Bed, taking into account the fact that this formula must then be copied into cells **G6** to **G19**; to calculate the share of the profit made by an article, divide the article's profit by the total profit made.

If you want to put what you have learnt into practice on a real document, you can work on summary exercise 4 for the CALCULATIONS section, that you can find at the end of this book.

It is often possible to perform a task in several different ways, but here, only the easiest solution is presented. You can go back to the corresponding lesson if you want to see other techniques you could use.

Solution to Exercise 4.1

1. To enter a formula in cell F5 that will multiply the Profit Margin by the Quantity, click cell **F5**.
Type an = sign, click cell **D5**, type an * sign then click cell **E5**.
Press the ⏎ key to enter the formula.

   To copy the content of cell F5 onto cells F6 to F19, click in cell **F5**.
Point to the fill handle on cell **F5**, then drag it down to cell **F19**.

2. To alter the formula in cell D13 to subtract the Cost Price of the Rectangular table from the Sale Price of the same product, double-click cell **D13** then delete the reference to cell **B14**.
Click cell **B13** to add the **B13** cell reference to the formula then confirm your changes by pressing ⏎.

3. To calculate the total Profit Made in cell F20 using AutoSum, click cell **F20**.

   Click the Σ tool button, make sure cells **F5:F19** are selected then press the ⏎ key to confirm.

4. To calculate the Share of profit made by the Sofa bed in cell G5, click cell **G5**.
Type =, click cell **F5**, press the / key, click cell **F20** then press the F4 key.
Press ⏎ to confirm your entry.

   To copy the formula in cell G5 into cells G6 to G19, click cell **G5**.
Point to the fill handle on cell **G5**, and drag it down to cell **G19**.

CALCULATIONS
Exercise 4.1: Formulas

CALCULATIONS
Lesson 4.2: Functions

📖 1 ▪ Using simple statistical functions 142

📖 2 ▪ Inserting a function with help from Excel..................................... 143

📖 3 ▪ Inserting a function manually 145

📖 4 ▪ Using the PMT financial function 146

📖 5 ▪ Making calculations on date type data.. 147

📖 6 ▪ Using 3-D references for cells and ranges................................... 148

Practice Exercise 4.2 149

CALCULATIONS
Lesson 4.2: Functions

▤1 ▪ Using simple statistical functions

- ※ Click the cell where the result will be displayed.

- ※ Open the list on the $\boxed{\Sigma \ \cdot}$ tool button by clicking the black arrow.

- ※ Click the required function:

Average	to calculate the average of a set of cells.
Count	to count up within a set of cells the number of cells containing numerical values.
Max	to extract the highest value from a group of cells.
Min	to extract the lowest value from a group of cells.

IF	▼ ✗ ✓ ƒₓ =AVERAGE(C6:C12)			
	A	B	C	D	E
2	**Orders 14 June**				
3					
4					
5		Quantity	Unit Price	Total	
6	Red & Black Whisky	9	14.50	130.50	
7	Bordeaux 1999 Red	2	3.20	6.40	
8	Queen's Gin	4	11.00	44.00	
9	Wild Chicken Bourbon	5	11.60	58.00	
10	Smirchoff Vodka	8	19.50	156.00	
11	White Vermouth	4	7.80	31.20	
12					
13	Average unit price	=AVERAGE(C6:C12)			
14		AVERAGE(**number1**, [number2], ...)			
15					

Excel displays your chosen function and selects a group of cells as a suggestion.

- ※ If the suggested selection is incorrect, modify it by clicking to select a cell or dragging to select a range of cells.

- ※ Confirm the formula by pressing the ⏎ key.

▌142

🕮2 ▪ Inserting a function with help from Excel

» Click the cell where the result will be displayed.

» Click the [fx] button on the formula bar or use the **Insert - Function** command.

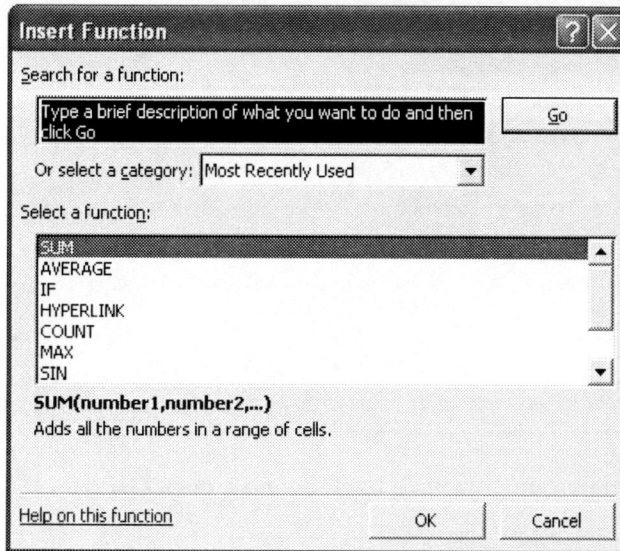

» To look for a particular function, you can use the **Search for a function** box: enter either the name of the function or a brief description of what you need the function to do then click **Go** to start searching.

» The **Or select a category** list displays the functions grouped by category.

*The **Most Recently Used** category shows the last functions you have used as well as the most frequently used ones. The **All** category displays all the available functions.*

» Choose your required function from the **Select a function** list.

» Click **OK** to open the **Function Arguments** dialog box.

▪ To set each argument within the function:

   - click the corresponding text box and click the ▨ button,

   - on the worksheet, select the cell(s) corresponding to the argument,

   - click ▨ to restore the dialog box.

▪ When all the arguments have been defined, click **OK**.

📄 *You can also insert a function within a formula or within another function. To do this, start the formula and at the appropriate place click the* ▼ *button on the formula bar. This displays a list of the last functions used and the* ***More Functions*** *option which takes you to a full list of functions.*

If you know the formula you want to use, you can enter it directly into the cell. If you do this, a ScreenTip appears, showing the different arguments you must set.

▦3 ▪ Inserting a function manually

To insert a function without any help from Excel, you simply type in all the function's arguments, following the syntax faultlessly. The example below uses the IF function, which is a logical function that obtains a result by setting one or more conditions.

▪ Activate the cell that should display the result.

▪ Type the = sign then the name of the required function.

The syntax of the function appears in a ScreenTip.

▪ In this example, set a condition respecting this syntax:
=IF(condition,action_if_condition_is_met,action_if_condition_is_not_met)

C3	▼	*fx* =IF(B3>=10,"Pass","")	
	A	B	C
1			
2	**Student Name**	**Marks**	**Final Result**
3	Anna Higgins	15	Pass
4	Gavin Myers	8	
5	Elena Marinov	7	
6	Stephen Carter	11	Pass
7	Sarah Fitton	17	Pass
8			

If the value in cell B3 equals or is greater than 10, the text "Pass" is shown in the result cell; otherwise, nothing appears in the cell (here, the formula has been copied into cells C3 to C7).

📄 *In a conditional formula, a variety of actions can be performed:*

Displaying a number	enter the number,
Displaying a text	enter the text between quotation marks,
Displaying the result of a calculation	enter the calculation formula,
Displaying the contents of a cell	select the cell,
Displaying zero	enter nothing,
No display	type "".

For conditions, several operators are available:

>/<	greater than/less than,
<>	different from,
>=/<=	greater than or equal to/less than or equal to.

To set several conditions, use one of the following functions, depending on the desired result. If several conditions should be met simultaneously:
=IF(AND(cond1,cond2,...,condn),action to be carried out if all the conditions are satisfied,action to be carried out if any condition is not satisfied)
If at least one condition must be met:
=IF(OR(cond1,cond2,...,condn),action to be carried out if at least one condition is satisfied,action to be carried out if no condition is satisfied)
If several conditions are nested (one in the other):
=IF(cond1,action if TRUE,IF(cond2,action if TRUE,IF(cond3,action if TRUE, action if FALSE)))

4 ▪ Using the PMT financial function

This function calculates the repayments on a loan, based on constant payments and interest rate.

▪ Click the cell in which you want to display the result.

▪ Make your calculation, following this syntax:

=PMT(rate,nper,pv,fv,type)

rate	refers to the interest rate of the loan.
nper	is the total number of payments to be made.
pv	is the loan principal or the total value that the series of payments is worth now.
fv	is the future value, or the balance obtained after the last payment.
type	indicates when each payment should be made: 1 if it is made at the beginning of the period or 0 if it is made at the end of the period.

The **fv** and **type** arguments are optional. If you do not include them, a default value of 0 (zero) is taken into account.

❋ Press the ⏎ key to confirm.

The result obtained includes only the loan principal and the interest due; it does not calculate any charges or deposits.

If you want to display a positive value, place a minus sign (-) in front of the function name, for example =- **PMT( )**.

> It is important to use the same unit for the rate and nper arguments. For example, if you are making monthly repayments on a loan over five years with an interest rate of 6%, you should use 6%/12 for the rate and 5*12 for nper (which calculates on the basis of monthly payments). If you are making annual payments, use 6% for the rate and 5 for nper.

> If you insert a function with help from Excel in the form of the **Function Arguments** dialog box (cf. Lesson 4.2 - 2. Inserting a function with help from Excel), you can see a description of each argument and the result of the calculation in the bottom of the dialog box.
> To calculate the total amount paid over the duration of the loan, simply multiply the result of the PMT formula by the nper value.

⊞5 ▪ Making calculations on date type data

❋ If the calculation refers to days, continue as for any other calculation, as the result of date calculations always appears as a number of days.

❋ To add months to a start date, use the following syntax:
=DATE(YEAR(start_date),MONTH(start_date)+period_in_months,DAY(start_date))

To add a number of years, use:
=DATE(YEAR(start_date)+period_in_years,MONTH(start_date),DAY(start_date))

CALCULATIONS
Lesson 4.2: Functions

For example, to calculate the date 2 months from now, use:
=DATE(YEAR(TODAY()),MONTH(TODAY())+2,DAY(TODAY()))

📄 *If the results of your calculations are four years ahead of what they ought to be, deactivate the **1904 date system** option in **Tools - Options - Calculation** tab.*

You can insert the system date into a cell by using the **TODAY()** or **NOW()** functions (cf. Lesson 3.1 - 1. Entering constants).

📖6 ▪ Using 3-D references for cells and ranges

A 3-D reference is a cell reference that includes the worksheet name, which you can use to analyse data in the <u>same cell</u> or the <u>same cell range</u> in <u>several different worksheets</u> in a workbook.

▪ Activate the cell where you want to display the result.

▪ Start your formula with an equals sign (=) and the name of the function you want to use: you can also insert the function with the [fx] tool button (cf. 4.2 - 2. Inserting a function with help from Excel).

▪ Enter the 3-D reference along this syntax: **start name:end name!cell** then continue building your formula.

For example, *=AVERAGE(**Sheet1:Sheet3!C3**)*.

This formula calculates the average of the values contained in cell **C3** over all the worksheets between **Sheet1** and **Sheet3**, inclusive.

📄 *A 3-D reference can be used in the process of defining names (**Insert - Name - Define**) and in formulas using the following functions: SUM, AVERAGE, AVERAGEA, COUNT, COUNTA, MAX, MAXA, MIN, MINA, PRODUCT, STDEV, STDEVA, STDEVP, STDEVPA, VAR, VARA, VARP, and VARPA.*

However, you cannot use a 3-D function in an array formula.

Below, you can see **Practice Exercise** 4.2. This exercise is made up of 6 steps. If you do not know how to do one of the steps, go back to the title that corresponds to that particular lesson. When you have finished, you can check your work by reading the **Solution** that follows.

All the steps in this exercise are likely to be tested in the MOUS exam.

☞ Practice Exercise 4.2

1. In **Sheet1** of the **4-2 Furniture.xls** workbook, which is in the **MOUS Excel 2002** folder, use common statistical functions to perform these tasks:

   - calculate the average profit made, in cell **B22**,

   - extract the best profit made into cell **B23**,

   - extract the lowest profit made into cell **B24**.

2. Using the **Insert Function** feature, enter a formula in cell **H6** on **Sheet1** in the **4-2 HiFi.xls** workbook, in the **MOUS Excel 2002** folder, that will display the text **Below Objective** if the total for January is less than 10,000. If the January total is greater than or equal to 10,000, the text **Above Objective** should be displayed.

   Copy this formula into cells **H7** to **H17**.

3. Set a condition in cell **I6** on **Sheet1** in the **4-2 HiFi.xls** workbook that will calculate a 5% commission on the Monthly Total, if this amount is less than or equal to 10,000, or a 10% commission on the Monthly Total if this amount is greater than 10,000. Copy this formula into cells **I7** to **I17**.

4. In cell **C14** on the **Taylor** worksheet in the **4-2 Loan.xls** workbook, calculate the value of each monthly repayment on the loan, using the **PMT** financial function. The end result should be displayed in positive figures.

🖽 5. In cell **C16** on the **Taylor** worksheet in the **4-2 Loan.xls** workbook, calculate the date of the last repayment of the loan.

🖽 6. On the **Average** sheet of the **4-2 Sales 1st Quarter.xls** workbook, in the **MOUS Excel 2002** folder, go to cell **B6** and use a 3-D reference to calculate the average monthly sales for **Sumner**, **Conroy** and **Farelli**. Copy this formula into cells **C6** and **D6**.

If you want to put what you have learnt into practice on a real document, you can work on summary exercise 4 for the CALCULATIONS section, that you can find at the end of this book.

It is often possible to perform a task in several different ways, but here, only the easiest solution is presented. You can go back to the corresponding lesson if you want to see other techniques you could use.

Solution to Exercise 4.2

1. Open the **4-2 Furniture.xls** workbook, which is in the **MOUS Excel 2002** folder, and if necessary, click the sheet tab of **Sheet1**.

   To calculate the average profit made in cell B22, click cell **B22**.

   Open the list on the $\boxed{\Sigma \ \cdot}$ tool button and click the **Average** function. Drag to select cells **F5** to **F19** and press ⏎ to confirm.

   To extract the best profit made into cell B23, click cell **B23**.

   Open the list on the $\boxed{\Sigma \ \cdot}$ tool button and click the **Max** function. Drag to select cells **F5** to **F19** and press ⏎ to confirm.

   To extract the lowest profit made into cell B24, click cell **B24**.

   Open the list on the $\boxed{\Sigma \ \cdot}$ tool button and click the **Min** function. Drag to select cells **F5** to **F19** and press ⏎ to confirm.

2. Open the **4-2 HiFi.xls** workbook in the **MOUS Excel 2002** folder, and if necessary, click the sheet tab of **Sheet1**.
   To use the Insert Function feature to enter a formula in cell H6 that will display the text "Below Objective" if the total for January is less than 10,000 or the text "Above Objective", if the January total is greater than or equal to 10,000, start by clicking cell **H6**.

   Click the $\boxed{fx}$ tool button on the formula bar.

   Delete any text that may be in the **Search for a function** box then enter **IF** and click the **Go** button next to the text box.

Click the **IF** function within the **Select a function** list and click **OK** at the bottom of the dialog box.

Click the ⬛ button in the **Logical_test** box, select the cell **E6**, type a < sign followed by **10000** then click the ⬛ button.

Click the **Value_if_true** box then type **Below Objective**.

Click the **Value_if_false** box then type **Above Objective**.

Confirm the formula by clicking **OK**.

Copy the formula by dragging the fill handle from cell **H6** over cells **H7** to **H17**.

3. To set a condition in cell I6 that will calculate a 5% commission on the Monthly Total, if this amount is less than or equal to 10,000, or a 10% commission on the Monthly Total if this amount is greater than 10,000, start by clicking cell **I6**.

Type this formula **=IF(E6<=10000,E6*5%,E6*10%)** into the cell and press ⬛ to confirm.
Copy the formula by dragging the fill handle from cell **I6** over cells **I7** to **I17**.

4. To calculate, in cell C14 on the Taylor worksheet in 4-2 Loan.xls, the value of each monthly repayment on the loan, open the **4-2 Loan.xls** workbook and click the **Taylor** sheet tab then cell **C14**.
Type **=-PMT(C11/12,C12,C10)** and confirm with ⬛.

The total should be 966.64.

5. To calculate in cell C16 on the Taylor worksheet in 4-2 Loan.xls, the date of the last repayment of the loan, click cell **C16**.

Type **=DATE(2002,1+60,1)** and confirm with ⬛.

The date calculated is 1 January 2007.

6. To use a 3-D reference to calculate average monthly sales in cell B6 on the Average sheet in 4-2 Sales 1st Quarter.xls, open the **4-2 Sales 1st Quarter.xls** workbook, in the **MOUS Excel 2002** folder, and click the **Average** sheet tab then cell **B6**. In this cell, type **=AVERAGE(Sumner: Farelli!B10)** and press ⏎ to confirm.

Copy this formula to cells **C6** and **D6** by dragging the fill handle on cell **B6** over these cells.

PRESENTATION OF DATA
Lesson 5.1: Formatting data

1 ▪ Modifying font and/or size of characters 156

2 ▪ Modifying font colour 157

3 ▪ Modifying text attributes 157

4 ▪ Formatting numerical values 158

5 ▪ Formatting dates/times 160

6 ▪ Aligning cell contents horizontally 160

7 ▪ Aligning cell contents vertically 161

8 ▪ Copying formats 162

9 ▪ Applying an AutoFormat to a table 162

10 ▪ Modifying cell borders 163

11 ▪ Applying colour to the background of a cell 167

12 ▪ Applying a pattern to the background of a cell 167

13 ▪ Merging cells 168

14 ▪ Modifying the orientation of text 169

15 ▪ Indenting text in a cell 170

Practice Exercise 5.1 172

PRESENTATION OF DATA
Lesson 5.1: Formatting data

▦1 ▪ Modifying font and/or size of characters

▪ Select the cells or data concerned. If you wish to select only some of the characters contained in a cell, select those characters in the formula bar.

▪ Select the font and font size in the first two list boxes on the **Formatting** toolbar:

Fonts that display a TT symbol are True Type fonts managed by Windows.

▪ To define the default font and font size for any new workbook, use **Tools - Options - General** tab (**Standard font** and **Size** options). These changes will take effect only when you restart Excel.

> 📄 *You can also use the options in **Format - Cells - Font** tab to change the font or font size used.*

⊞2 ▪ **Modifying font colour**

▪ Select the cells or data concerned.

▪ Open the drop-down list on the [**A** ▾] tool button on the **Formatting** toolbar, by clicking the black triangle.

▪ Click the colour you wish to use.

> *The colour selected is then displayed on the button itself. To apply this colour to any piece of text, you only have to click the button, without opening the list again.*
>
> *You can also select the font **Color** in the **Format Cells** dialog box (**Format - Cells - Font** tab).*

⊞3 ▪ **Modifying text attributes**

▪ Select the cells or data concerned.

▪ Choose between:

[**B**] or ⌂ Ctrl **B** to apply a **bold** typeface.

[***I***] or ⌂ Ctrl **I** to apply *italics*.

[**U**] or ⌂ Ctrl **U** to apply <u>underlining</u>.

> *If you repeat the same command for the same text, you cancel the corresponding attribute.*
>
> *You can apply more than one attribute to the same text.*

PRESENTATION OF DATA
Lesson 5.1: Formatting data

▢ ▪ Select the cells or data concerned.

▪ **Format - Cells** or ⌨ **1**

▪ Click the **Font** tab.

▪ Activate all the formats to be applied to the text.

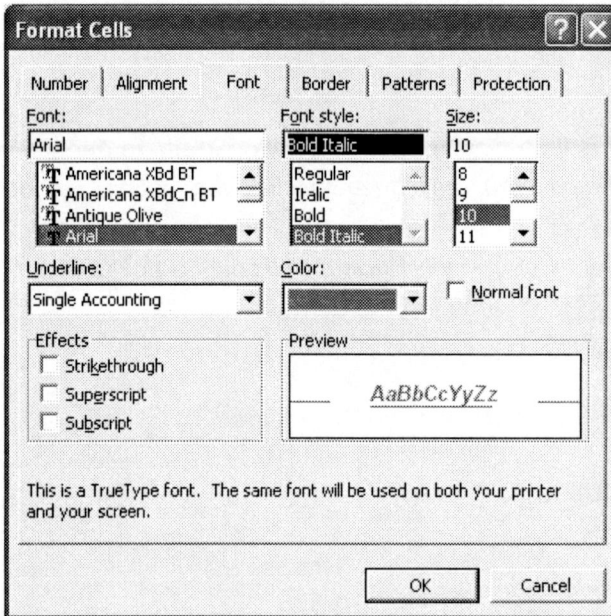

*The three options in the **Effects** frame and some of the **Underline** options are all options that are available only through the menus.*

▪ Click **OK**.

▦4 ▪ Formatting numerical values

▢ ▪ Select the values concerned.

▪ **Format - Cells**

▪ Click the **Number** tab.

▪ In the **Category** list, select the category of format you wish to use.

158

- If necessary, change the options for the format (such as the number of decimal places).

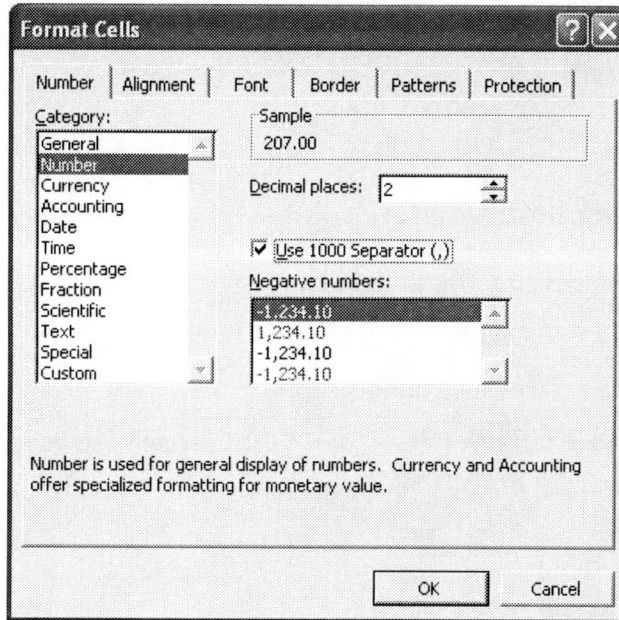

- Click **OK**.

- Select the values concerned.

- Choose one of the following formats:

[icon]	Currency	(£10,000.00 or $10,000.00, depending on your Regional Settings)
[icon]	Euro	(€10 000,00)
[icon]	Percent	(100000%)
[icon]	Comma	(10,000.00)

PRESENTATION OF DATA
Lesson 5.1: Formatting data

📄 *Hash symbols may appear in some cells if the column width is insufficient to display the requested format.*

To add a decimal place, click 🔲*; to use one less decimal place, click* 🔲*.*

📖5 ▪ Formatting dates/times

- Select the values you wish to format.
- **Format - Cells** or ⌨ **Ctrl 1**
- If necessary, activate the **Number** tab.
- Select the **Date** or **Time** format type in the **Category** list, as required.
- Select the desired format in the **Type** list.
- Click **OK**.

📖6 ▪ Aligning cell contents horizontally

Horizontal alignment is calculated according to the width of each column.

🖱 ▪ Select the cells concerned.
- Click one of the following three tools:

  🔲 align on the left

  🔲 centre

  🔲 align on the right.

- Select the cells concerned.

- **Format - Cells** or Ctrl 1

- Click the **Alignment** tab.

- Select the required alignment from the **Horizontal** list box.

- To indent contents within a cell, give the indent to apply to the left edge of the cell in the **Indent** box.

- Click **OK**.

7 ▪ Aligning cell contents vertically

Vertical alignment is defined with reference to the row height.

- Select the cells concerned.

- **Format - Cells** or Ctrl 1

- Click the **Alignment** tab.

- Select the required alignment from the **Vertical** list box.

- Click **OK**.

You can spread a cell entry over the height of the cell, keeping the same column width but adjusting the height of the cell: to do this, select the cell(s) concerned then use ***Format - Cells - Alignment*** *tab, activate the* ***Wrap text*** *option and click* ***OK***.

8 ▪ Copying formats

This technique uses the format painter tool to copy the presentation of one cell range onto another.

▪ Select the cell(s) containing the format you want to copy.

▪ Click the 🖌 tool button.

The pointer takes the form of a paintbrush.

▪ Select the cells that are to take the copied format.

> 🖌 *If you wish to copy the format onto several different places, select the 🖌 tool with a double-click. Press* Esc *to deactivate the format painter.*

🎏9 ▪ Applying an AutoFormat to a table

▪ Select the table you wish to format.

▪ **Format - AutoFormat**

▪ In the list of AutoFormats, choose the most suitable style.

▪ To see options about which formatting features will be applied, click the **Options** button.

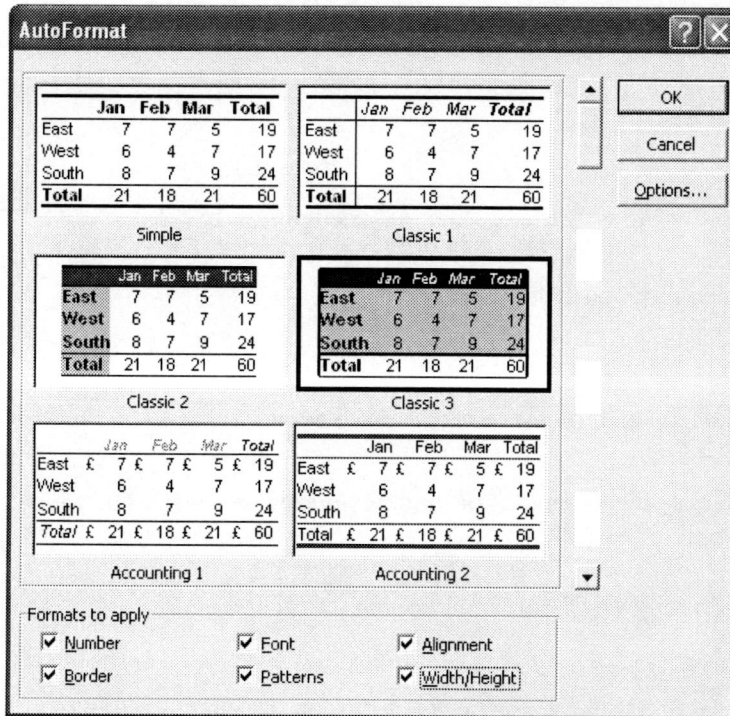

» If necessary deactivate any formats that you do not wish Excel to apply.

» Click **OK**.

10 ▪ **Modifying cell borders**

Applying borders

» Select the cells concerned.

» Open the [ ] list by clicking the black arrow.

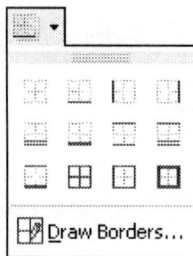

- Click the required style of border.

The *tool button now shows a picture of the last border style chosen.*

- Deselect to see the new border more clearly.

> *To apply coloured or noncontinuous borders, you must use the menu options.*
>
> *To remove all borders, click the* *button.*

> *To apply the same border to another selection of cells, you can click the tool button without opening the list.*

- Select the cells concerned.
- **Format - Cells** or [Ctrl] **1**
- Click the **Border** tab.
- To put a border all around the edge of the selection, choose the **Style** and **Color** of the border then click the **Outline** button.
- To place a border along one or more edges of the selection, choose first a **Style** and **Color** then in the **Border** frame, click the buttons corresponding to the borders you wish to display or hide. Click the **Inside** button to apply the border to the edges of each individual cell in the selection.

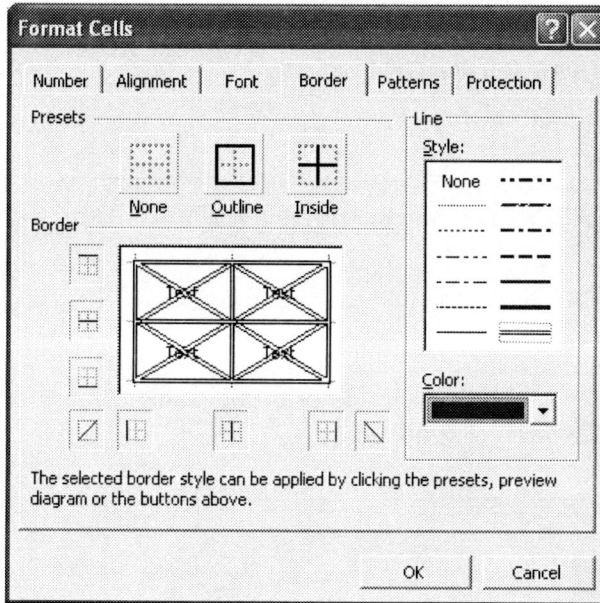

The [icon] *and* [icon]
buttons are used to draw diagonal lines through cells.

* Confirm by clicking **OK**.
* Show the result by clicking outside the selected cells.

Drawing borders

* Open the [icon] list by clicking the black arrow.
* Click the **Draw Borders** option.

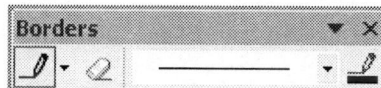

*The **Borders** toolbar appears and the mouse pointer takes the shape of a pencil.*

PRESENTATION OF DATA
Lesson 5.1: Formatting data

▪ The default drawing mode is **Draw Border** which draws an outline around the selected area. If you wish to draw inside gridlines instead, open the list on the [✎▾] tool and choose the **Draw Border Grid** option.

*When you choose **Draw Border Grid** mode, the pencil pointer is accompanied by a small grid.*

▪ If required, open the [────── ▾] list and choose a line style.

▪ Click [✎] if you want to select another colour.

▪ To draw a border along one edge of a range of cells, drag along that edge.

▪ To draw a border around the outside of a range or a grid within a range, drag from the starting cell up to the last cell required.

	A	B	C	D	E
1					
2	Orders 14 June	Borders		▾ ✕	
3		✎⊞ ▾ ✎	──────	▾ ✎	
4					
5		Quantity	Unit Price	Total	
6	Red & Black Whisky	9	14.50	130.50	
7	Bordeaux 1999 Red	2	3.20	6.40	
8	Queen's Gin	4	11.00	44.00	
9	Wild Chicken Bourbon	5	11.60	58.00	
10	Smirchoff Vodka	8	19.50	156.00	
11	White Vermouth	4	7.80	31.20	✎⊞
12					

▪ To remove one or more borders, click the [✎] tool button (the pointer becomes an eraser) and drag along the borders you wish to erase.

▪ To deactivate the border drawing mode, press [Esc] or click the [✎] tool button again.

▪ If you no longer need it, close the **Borders** toolbar by clicking its [✕] button.

*While you are using **Draw Border** mode, you can temporarily switch to **Draw Border Grid** mode by holding down the ⌊Ctrl⌋ key. Holding down the ⌊Shift⌋ key switches to erasing mode, with the pointer becoming an eraser temporarily.*

11 ▪ Applying colour to the background of a cell

▪ Select the cells you wish to colour.

▪ Open the [▧ ▾] list by clicking the black arrow.

▪ Click the required colour.

The [▧ ▾] tool button shows the last colour chosen. Click this button (without opening the list) to apply this same colour to other selected cells.

▪ Click outside the selection to see the results clearly.

*You can also use the **Color** list on the **Patterns** tab of the **Format Cells** dialog box (**Format - Cells**) to change the colour of cells.*

12 ▪ Applying a pattern to the background of a cell

▪ Select the cells concerned.

▪ **Format - Cells** or ⌊Ctrl⌋ 1

▪ Click the **Patterns** tab.

▪ If necessary, choose a **Color** for the cell background.

▪ Open the **Pattern** list to choose a pattern type and a pattern colour.

PRESENTATION OF DATA
Lesson 5.1: Formatting data

- Click **OK**.
- Show the result by clicking outside the selected cells.

13 ▪ Merging cells

Cells that have been merged become a single cell:

The text ORDERS belongs to cell A6 but appears over cells A6 to A11, which are merged.

- Select the cells concerned.

  Only the data in the first cell of the selection (at the top left of the range of cells) will appear in the merged cells.

- **Format - Cells** or [Ctrl] 1

- Click the **Alignment** tab.

- Activate the **Merge cells** option.

- If necessary, specify the **Text alignment** that you wish to apply to the data in the merged cells.

- Click **OK**.

  The [icon] button merges selected cells (provided that they are in the same row) and centres the data in the first cell across the merged cells.

  To split cells that have been merged, select the merged cell and click the [icon] tool button again.

14 ▪ Modifying the orientation of text

- Select the cells concerned.

- **Format - Cells** or [Ctrl] 1

- Click the **Alignment** tab.

- In the **Orientation** frame, drag the horizontal word **Text** to define the rotation angle. You can also define this angle by changing the value in the **Degrees** box.

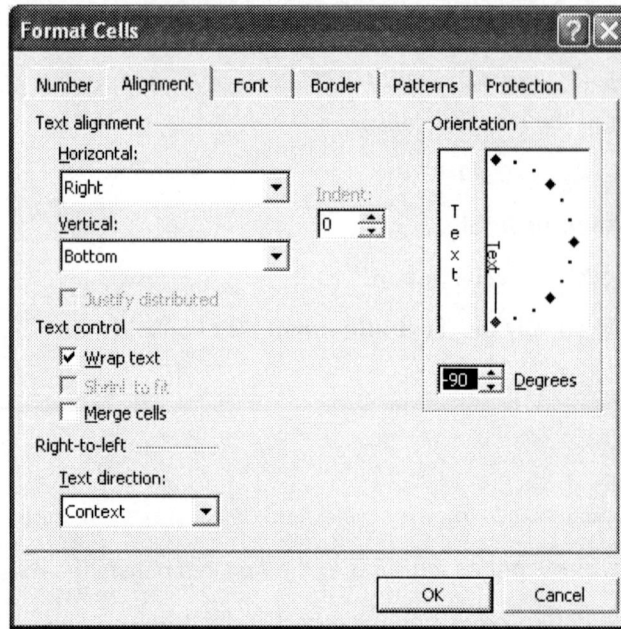

■ Click **OK**.

    *If you wish to place characters vertically, one beneath the other, click the vertical **Text** box in the **Orientation** frame.*

15 ▪ Indenting text in a cell

■ Select the cells concerned.

■ **Format - Cells** or ⌨ **1**

■ Click the **Alignment** tab.

■ In the **Horizontal** list, select the **Left (Indent)**, **Right (Indent)** or **Distributed (Indent)** option (the latter option gives a left and right indent).

* In the **Indent** text box, select or enter the indent value required (expressed as a number of characters).

* Click **OK**.

You can also indent text in a cell by clicking the [⊟] tool button to decrease the indent by one character or the [⊟] tool button to increase the indent by one character.

PRESENTATION OF DATA
Exercise 5.1: Formatting data

Below, you can see **Practice Exercise** 5.1. This exercise is made up of 15 steps. If you do not know how to do one of the steps, go back to the title that corresponds to that particular lesson. When you have finished, you can check your work by reading the **Solution** that follows.

Steps that are likely to be tested during the MOUS exam are marked with this symbol: ⊞. However, it is a good idea to complete the whole exercise to ensure you have understood everything covered in the lesson.

☞ Practice Exercise 5.1

---

*To work on exercise 5.1, you should open the **5-1 Furniture.xls** workbook located in the **MOUS Excel 2002** folder and activate, if necessary, **Sheet1**.*

⊞ 1. In cell **A1**, modify the character font to **Arial Black** and the font size to **12**.

⊞ 2. Modify the colour of the characters in cell **A1** to **red**.

⊞ 3. Make the following formatting changes:
   - Put cells **B4** to **G4** then cells **A22** to **A25** in **bold** type.
   - Put the characters in cell **A1** in italics.
   - Underline the characters in cell **A28**.

⊞ 4. Apply a **Comma** style to cells **B5** to **D19**, then delete two decimal places from cells **B5** to **D19**.

⊞ 5. Format the date in cell **B28** in a **dd mmmm yyyy** format (for example: 26 December 2001).

⊞ 6. Centre the contents of cells **B4** to **G4** horizontally.

⊞ 7. Centre the contents of cells **B4** to **G4** vertically.

8. Copy the formatting of cell **B4** onto cell **A4**.

🗗 9. To cells **A22** to **B25** apply a **Classic 3** AutoFormat; the alignment and cell width and height should not be modified.

10. Put borders around cells **A4** to **G20** following the illustration below:

PRODUCT	COST PRICE	SALE PRICE	PROFIT MARGIN	QUANTITY	PROFIT MADE	SHARE OF PROFIT
Sofa bed	207	258.75	51.75	25	1294	4%
Sofa (3 seater)	449	538.8	89.8	18	1616	5%
Single bed	199	238.8	39.8	42	1672	5%
Double bed	399	518.7	119.7	58	6943	21%
Dining chair	45	58.5	13.5	57	770	2%
Folding chair	26	33.8	7.8	120	936	3%
Coffee table	141	183.3	42.3	14	592	2%
Square table	98	127.4	29.4	48	1411	4%
Rectangular table	326	423.8	97.8	22	2152	6%
Wardrobe 2 door	228	296.4	68.4	21	1436	4%
Buffet 2 door	360	450	90	65	5850	17%
Buffet 3 door	460	575	115	37	4255	13%
Dresser 3 drawers	112	140	28	45	1260	4%
Bookshelf large	157	204.1	47.1	30	1413	4%
Bookshelf small	114	148.2	34.2	57	1949	6%
TOTAL					33549	100%

11. Apply a **Gray - 25%** background colour to cells **A4** to **G4** and **A20** to **G20**.

12. Apply this pattern: ⬚ to the background of cells **A4** to **G4** and **A20** to **G20**.

🗗 13. Merge cells **A1** to **G1** and, simultaneously, centre the content of **A1** across columns A to G.

14. Apply a **-90% Degrees** orientation to the text in cell **A4**.

15. Apply a left indent, two characters wide, in cells **A5** to **A19**.

If you want to put what you have learnt into practice on a real document, you can work on summary exercise 6 for the PRESENTATION OF DATA section that you can find at the end of this book.

Exercise 5.1: Formatting data

It is often possible to perform a task in several different ways, but here, only the easiest solution is presented. You can go back to the corresponding lesson if you want to see other techniques you could use.

Solution to Exercise 5.1

1. To modify the font in cell A1 to Arial Black and the font size to **12**, click cell **A1**.
   Open the **Font** list box on the **Formatting** toolbar then click the **Arial Black** font.
   Open the **Font Size** list box on the **Formatting** toolbar then click a size of **12**.

2. To put the characters in cell A1 in red, click cell **A1**.
   Open the list on the [A ▾] tool button then click the red colour.

3. To put cells B4 to G4 then cells A22 to A25 in bold type, select cells **B4** to **G4** and hold down the [Ctrl] key and select cells **A22** to **A25**.
   Click the [B] tool button.

   To put the characters in cell A1 in italics, click cell **A1** then click the [I] tool button.

   To underline the characters in cell A28, click cell **A28** then the [U] tool button.

4. To apply a Comma style to cells B5 to D19, select cells **B5** to **D19** then click the [,] tool button. To delete two decimal places from cells B5 to D19, select cells **B5** to **D19** if necessary then click the [.00 →.0] tool button twice.

5. To put the date in cell B28 in a dd mmmm yyyy format, click cell **B28**, use the **Format - Cells** command then click the **Number** tab.
Select **Date** in the **Category** list then in the **Type** list, click *14 **March 2001**.
Confirm by clicking **OK**.

6. To centre the contents of cells B4 to G4 horizontally, select cells **B4** to **G4** then click the ▤ tool button.

7. To centre the contents of cells B4 to G4 vertically, select cells **B4** to **G4** and use the **Format - Cells** command. Click the **Alignment** tab.
Open the **Vertical** list box then click the **Center** option.
Click **OK** to confirm.

8. To copy the format of cell B4 to cell A4, select cell **B4**. Click the ▥ tool button then click cell **A4**.

9. To apply a Classic 3 AutoFormat to cells A22 to B25, without affecting the alignment or cell width/height, select cells **A22** to **B25**.
Use the **Format - AutoFormat** command then select the **Classic 3** format.
Click the **Options** button and deactivate the **Alignment** and **Width/Height** options then click **OK**.

10. To apply borders around cells A4 to G20, select cells **A4** to **G20**, open the list on the ▤▾ tool button and click the ▣ border type.

Select cells **A4** to **G4** and **A19** to **G19**, open the list on the ▤▾ tool button then click the ▤ border type.
Select cells **A4** to **G20**, use the **Format - Cells** command and click the **Border** tab. In the **Style** box, select the last line style in the first column, click the ▤ button in the **Border** frame then click **OK**.

Click outside the selection to see the result.

11. To apply a Gray -25% colour to cells A4 to G4 and A20 to G20, select cells **A4** to **G4** and **A20** to **G20**.

    Open the list on the tool button and click the **Gray - 25%** colour. Click outside the selection to see the result.

12. To apply a pattern to cells A4 to G4 and A20 to G20, select cells **A4** to **G4** and **A20** to **G20**.
    Use the **Format - Cells** command then click the **Patterns** tab.

    Open the **Pattern** list, click the pattern style then click **OK**. Click outside the selection to see the result.

13. To merge and centre cells A1 to G1 simultaneously, select cells **A1** to **G1** then click the tool button.

14. To apply a -90 degrees orientation to the text in cell A4, click cell **A4** to select it, use the **Format - Cells** command then click the **Alignment** tab. Type **-90** in the **Degrees** box then click **OK**.

15. To make a two-character left indent in cells A5 to A19, select cells **A5** to **A19** then click the tool twice.

PRESENTATION OF DATA
Lesson 5.2: Styles

1 ▪ Creating a style.. 178

2 ▪ Applying a style 179

3 ▪ Managing existing styles 179

Practice Exercise 5.2 181

1 ▪ Creating a style

Creating a style is a useful way of saving a certain group of attributes that you want to be able to apply quickly to other cells.

▪ Activate the cell whose formatting is to be saved as a style.

▪ **Format - Style** or ⌊Alt⌋ '

▪ Enter a new **Style name** for the style you are creating.

*A description of the style is displayed in the **Style Includes (By Example)** frame.*

▪ Deactivate any attributes that you do not want to include in the style.

▪ If necessary, use the **Modify** button to change some of the style's attributes before saving it.

▪ Click **OK**.

Styles are defined only for the active workbook.

2 ▪ Applying a style

- ▪ Select the cells to be formatted.
- ▪ **Format - Style** or [Alt] ,
- ▪ In the **Style name** list, select the style you want to use.
- ▪ Click **OK**.

3 ▪ Managing existing styles

Modifying a style

- ▪ **Format - Style** or [Alt] ,
- ▪ Select the style you want to modify in the **Style name** list.
- ▪ Click the **Modify** button.
- ▪ Make any changes then click **OK**.
- ▪ Click **OK** again.

  This immediately modifies all the cells to which the style was applied.

Deleting a style

- ▪ **Format - Style** or [Alt] ,
- ▪ Select the **Style name** you want to delete then click the **Delete** button.
- ▪ Click **OK**.

  All the cells to which the style was applied lose the style's formatting and take on a standard format.

  Be careful: you cannot undo deleting a style.

Integrating styles from another workbook

▪ Open the workbook containing the styles and the workbook into which you wish to copy them and leave this workbook open.

▪ **Format - Style** or ⌨ Alt ´

▪ Click the **Merge** button.

▪ In the list of the open workbooks, double-click the workbook containing the styles you wish to use.

▪ To apply the style to selected cells, select the style and click **OK**.

Below, you can see **Practice Exercise** 5.2. This exercise is made up of 3 steps. If you do not know how to do one of the steps, go back to the title that corresponds to that particular lesson. When you have finished, you can check your work by reading the **Solution** that follows.

Steps that are likely to be tested during the MOUS exam are marked with this symbol: ▦. However, it is a good idea to complete the whole exercise to ensure you have understood everything covered in the lesson.

☞ Practice Exercise 5.2

*To work on exercise 5.2, you should open the **5-2 Sales Progression.xls** workbook located in the **MOUS Excel 2002** folder then activate the **Results** sheet if necessary.*

1. Using the presentation of cell **A1** to help you, create a style called **Title**.

▦ 2. Apply the **Title** style to cell **A1** of the **Progression** worksheet.

3. Modify the **Title** style to include an indigo font colour.

If you want to put what you have learnt into practice on a real document, you can work on summary exercise 5 for the PRESENTATION OF DATA section that you can find at the end of this book.

It is often possible to perform a task in several different ways, but here, only the easiest solution is presented. You can go back to the corresponding lesson if you want to see other techniques you could use.

Solution to Exercise 5.2

1. To create a Title style from the presentation of cell A1, click cell **A1** then use the **Format - Style** command.

   Type **Title** in the **Style name** box then click **OK**.

2. To apply the Title style to cell A1 on the Progression worksheet, click the **Progression** tab then cell **A1** and use the **Format - Style** command.

   Open the **Style name** list, select the **Title** style then click **OK**.

3. To add an indigo font colour to the Title style, use the **Format - Style** command.

   Select **Title** in the **Style name** list then click the **Modify** button.

   Click the **Font** tab and open the drop-down list on the **Color** option. Click the indigo colour.

   Click **OK** once, then click it again.

PRINTING
Lesson 6.1: Printing

1 ▪ Printing a workbook or part of a workbook.. 184

2 ▪ Creating and printing a print area 184

3 ▪ Setting the print options.. 185

4 ▪ Previewing a sheet before printing 186

5 ▪ Previewing a non-interactive Web page 188

Practice Exercise 6.1 190

PRINTING
Lesson 6.1: Printing

1 • Printing a workbook or part of a workbook

- To print the active worksheet, using the default print settings, activate the sheet concerned and click the [printer icon] tool button.

- To print a workbook, a group of sheets, a selection of cells and/or to modify the print settings, select the items you want to print, if necessary, then use the **File - Print** command or Ctrl **P**.

  *The **Print** dialog box opens.*

- Change the print settings as required (cf. Setting the print options) then click **OK** to start printing.

2 • Creating and printing a print area

You can define a range or several ranges of cells as a print area. When you ask Excel to print, it will print only this area which is useful if you do not wish to print an entire worksheet.

- Select the range to be printed.

- **File - Print Area - Set Print Area**

  *If you start printing (**File - Print** or [printer icon]) a worksheet containing a print area, only the print area will be printed.*

  *To cancel a print area, use **File - Print Area - Clear Print Area**.*

⊞3 ▪ Setting the print options

▪ **File - Print** or `Ctrl` **P**

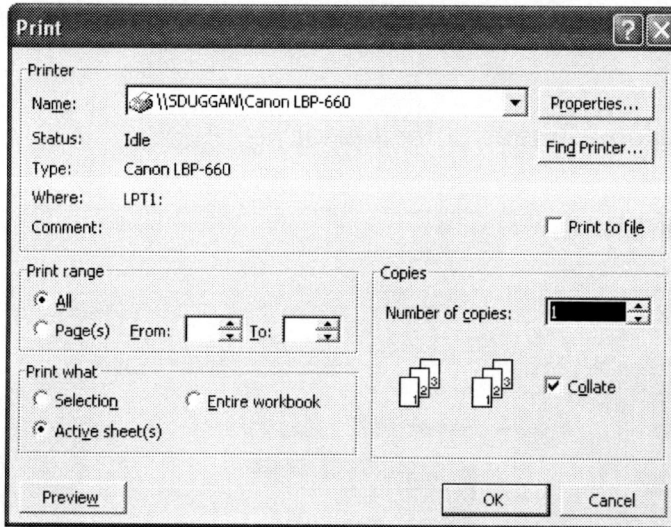

▪ The **Active sheet(s)** option, which is active by default in the **Print what** frame, prints the data from the active worksheet or any other sheets that happen to be selected.

▪ To print the range of cells selected in the active worksheet, choose the **Selection** option in the **Print what** frame.

▪ To print all the worksheets of the active workbook, select the **Entire workbook** option.

▪ To print a group of pages, click the **From** box and enter the number of the first page to print then enter the number of the last page in the **To** box.

▪ If you wish to make several copies of your work, enter the **Number of copies** required in the **Copies** frame.

*If you are printing several copies of a multiple page document, the **Collate** option prints one complete copy of the document after another.*

PRINTING
Lesson 6.1: Printing

📄 You can also access the **Print** dialog box by clicking the **Print** button when you are in the **Print Preview** window.

*If what you are printing is several pages wide or high, you can choose how to print these pages by using the **Down, then over** or **Over, then down** options in the **Page order** frame (**File - Page Setup - Sheet** tab).*

4 ▪ Previewing a sheet before printing

▪ **File - Print Preview** or 🔍

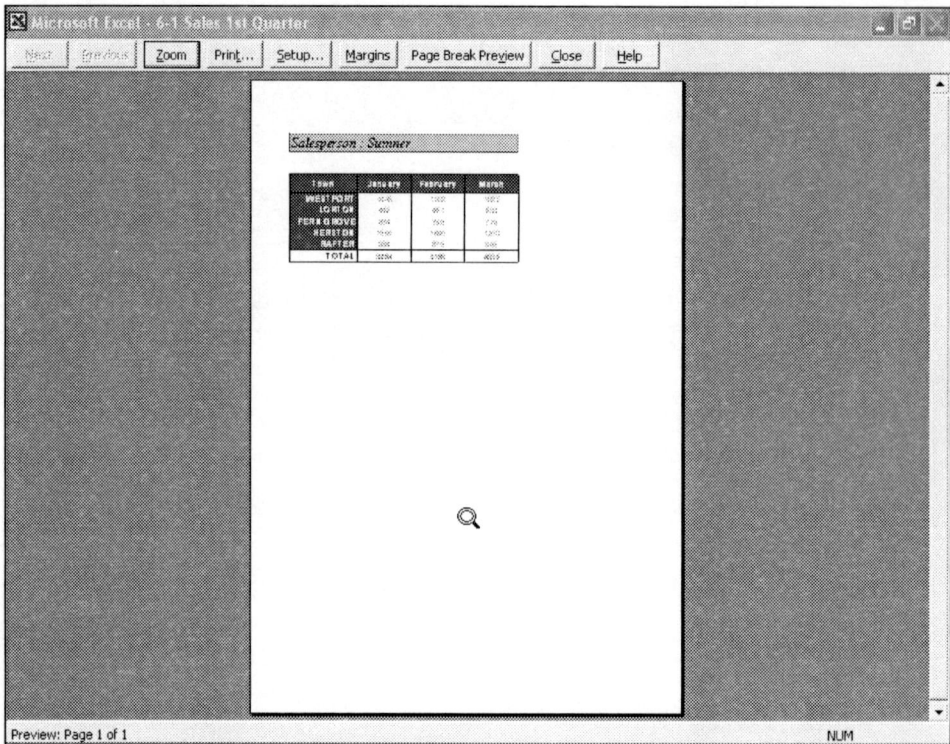

This produces a scaled-down view of the sheet, showing how it will look when printed. On the status bar, Excel displays the current page number and the total number of pages to be printed.

* To zoom in on a preview, place the mouse pointer on the item to be magnified and click.

Before you click, the mouse pointer appears as a magnifying glass; afterwards, it becomes an arrow.

* To return to the scaled-down preview, click the page again.

* To display another page, use the **Next** and **Previous** buttons.

In the scaled-down preview, you can also use the vertical scroll bar to change page.

* To modify margins and column widths, click the **Margins** button then drag the appropriate handle:

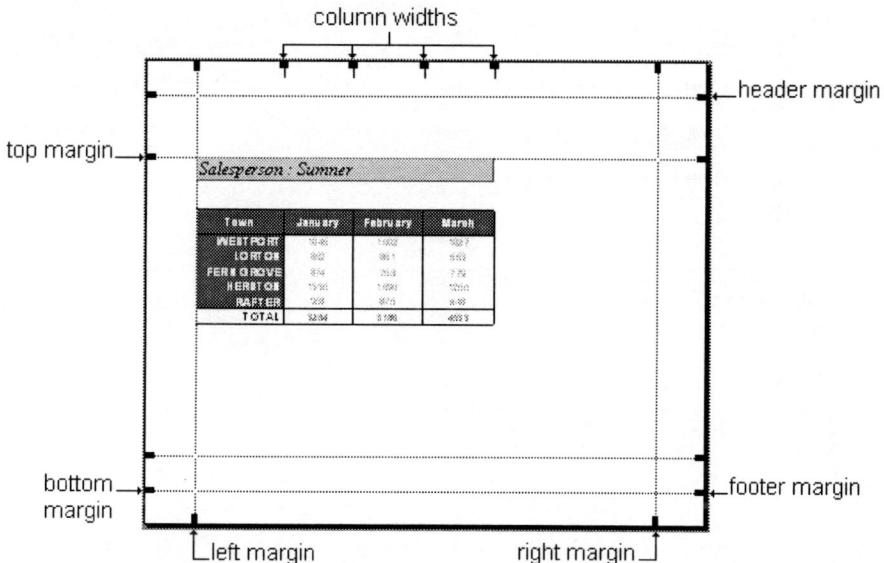

column widths

header margin

top margin

Salesperson : Sumner

Town	January	February	March
WESTPORT			
LORTON			
FERN GROVE			
HERBTON			
RAFTER			
TOTAL			

bottom margin

footer margin

left margin

right margin

* To start printing, click the **Print** button, check the print options then click **OK**.

* To leave the preview window, click the **Close** button or press Esc.

The **Page Break Preview** button makes the page breaks visible, so you reposition them.

📖5 ▪ Previewing a non-interactive Web page

▪ In Excel, open the workbook you wish to preview as a Web page (this can be a file in xls, htm or xml format, for example).

▪ **File - Web Page Preview**

The default Web browser opens and presents the Web page as *it would be seen on an intranet or the Internet.* By default, this renames the file by applying an htm extension to it (if the file is not already in htm format).

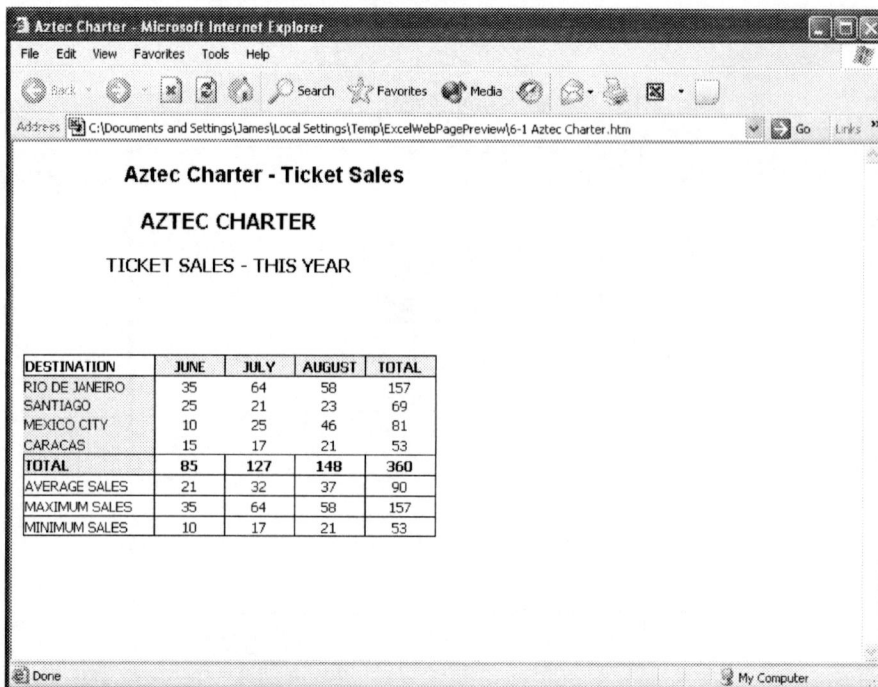

In this example, Internet Explorer 6 is the default browser.

* Close the browser once you have finished examining the page.

  The Excel application window reappears.

Below, you can see **Practice Exercise** 6.1. This exercise is made up of 5 steps. If you do not know how to do one of the steps, go back to the title that corresponds to that particular lesson. When you have finished, you can check your work by reading the **Solution** that follows.

All the steps in this exercise are likely to be tested in the MOUS exam.

Practice Exercise 6.1

1. Open the **6-1 Sales 1st Quarter.xls** workbook in the **MOUS Excel 2002** folder and print the **Sumner** worksheet.

2. Open the **6-1 HiFi.xls** workbook in the **MOUS Excel 2002** folder and on **Sheet1**, create a print area that takes in cells **A5** to **E18**. Next, print the print area you have created.

3. Open the **6-1 Furniture.xls** workbook in the **MOUS Excel 2002** folder and print three copies of the range of cells **A22** to **B25** on **Sheet1**.

4. Go to the **6-1 Sales 1st Quarter.xls** workbook and preview the **Sumner** worksheet in the print preview. Next, using the **Margins** button, set the top margin to **5 cm** (or about two inches).

5. Open the **6-1 Aztec Charter.htm** file and view it in a Web page preview.

If you want to put what you have learnt into practice on a real document, you can work on summary exercise 6 for the PRINTING section that you can find at the end of this book.

It is often possible to perform a task in several different ways, but here, only the easiest solution is presented. You can go back to the corresponding lesson if you want to see other techniques you could use.

Solution to Exercise 6.1

1. To print the Sumner workbook in the 6-1 Sales 1st Quarter.xls workbook, open the **6-1 Sales 1st Quarter.xls** workbook in the **MOUS Excel 2002** folder, click the **Sumner** sheet tab then click the 🖨 tool button.

2. To create a print area using cells A5 to E18 on Sheet1 of the 6-1HiFi.xls workbook, open the **6-1 HiFi.xls** workbook in the **MOUS Excel 2002** folder, then click the **Sheet1** sheet tab. Select cells **A5** to **E18** then use the **File - Print Area - Set Print Area** command.

   To print the print area you have just defined, click the 🖨 tool button.

3. To print three copies of the range of cells A22 to B25 on Sheet1 of the 6-1 Furniture.xls workbook, open the **6-1 Furniture.xls** workbook in the **MOUS Excel 2002** folder and click the **Sheet1** sheet tab.
   Select cells **A22** to **B25** then use the **File - Print** command.
   Click the **Selection** option in the **Print what** frame, enter **3** in the **Number of copies** box then click the **OK** button.

4. To see a print preview of the Sumner worksheet in the 6-1 Sales 1st Quarter.xls workbook, activate the **6-1 Sales 1st Quarter.xls** workbook (use the **Window** menu, for example) and click the **Sumner** sheet tab if necessary, then click the 🔍 tool button.

To set the top margin to 5 cm (or 2 inches), click the **Margins** button to display the margins then drag the second horizontal line downwards until you see the value **5** (or **2** if your unit of measurement is inches) appear on the status bar at the bottom of the Print Preview window.

5. To see a Web page preview of the 6-1 Aztec Charter.htm file, open the **6-1 Aztec Charter.htm** file in the **MOUS Excel 2002** folder then use the **File - Web Page Preview** command.

PRINTING
Lesson 6.2: Page Setup

📁 1 ▪ Modifying the page setup options 194

📁 2 ▪ Creating page headers and footers 197

📁 3 ▪ Repeating titles on each page 199

Practice Exercise 6.2 200

▦1 ▪ Modifying the page setup options

Accessing the page setup options

※ If you are in the print preview, click the **Setup** button.
Otherwise, use **File - Page Setup**.

Modifying page orientation

※ Go to the page setup options.

※ If necessary, activate the **Page** tab.

※ Choose the appropriate **Orientation**.

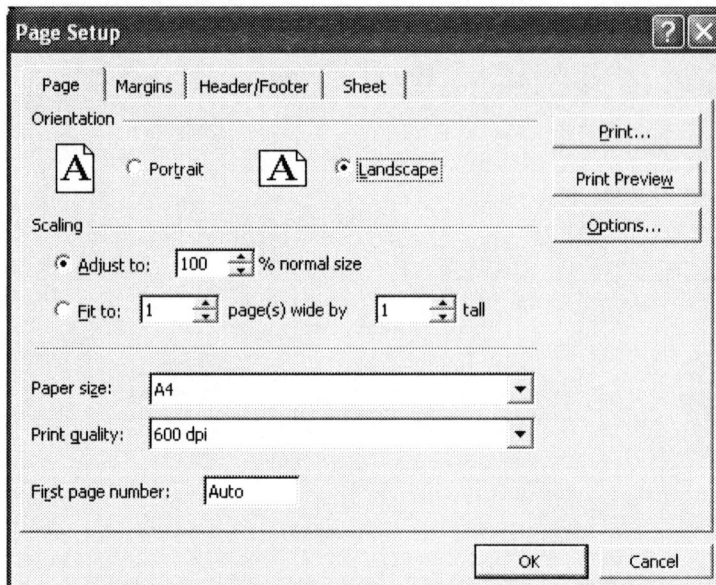

Portrait is also known as "Vertical" or "French". *Landscape* is also known as "Horizontal" or "Italian".

※ Click **OK**.

Changing the scale of printed pages

- Go to the page setup options.

- If necessary, activate the **Page** tab.

- In the **Adjust to** text box, under **Scaling**, give the scale you wish to apply as a percentage of the normal size.

- Click **OK**.

*If the **Fit to** option is active in the **Page Setup** dialog box (**Page** tab), Excel automatically adjusts the scale of printing so that the document fits the number of pages (in width/height) you specify.*

Printing a sheet with gridlines

- Go to the page setup options.

- If necessary, activate the **Sheet** tab.

- Activate the **Gridlines** option.

- Click **OK**.

Printing row and column headings

- Go to the page setup options.

- If necessary, activate the **Sheet** tab.

- Activate the **Row and column headings** option to print column letters and row numbers; deactivate this option if you do not want these to be printed.

- Click **OK**.

Printing comments and/or formula errors

▪ Go to the page setup options.

▪ If necessary, activate the **Sheet** tab.

▪ In the **Comments** list, select **At end of sheet** if you want to print a resume of the comments of a separate page or select **As displayed on sheet** to print the comments as they appear within the worksheet. When the **(None)** option is active, the comments will not be printed.

▪ In the **Cell errors as** list, choose how Excel should print any error values that appear in cells: **displayed**, to print the errors as they appear in the formula; **<blank>**, to print no error value; **--**, to print 2 dashes instead of the error values, or **#N/A**, to print the mention #N/A whatever the error value displayed.

Defining printing margins

▪ Go to the page setup options.

▪ If necessary, activate the **Margins** tab.

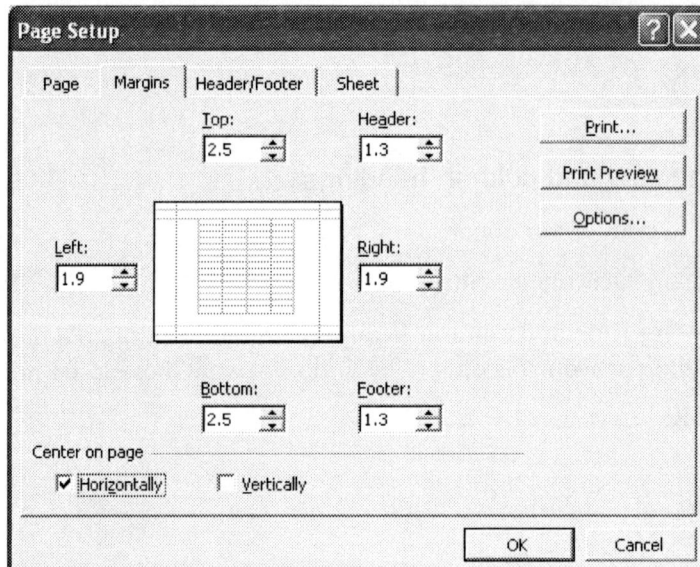

* Use the various text boxes to specify the corresponding margins. The **Header** and **Footer** options determine the position of the header text in the top margin and the footer text in the bottom margin.

* Activate the **Horizontally** and/or **Vertically** options to centre the table horizontally and/or vertically on the page.

* Click **OK**.

▪ Creating page headers and footers

The header is printed at the top of each page and the footer at the bottom of each page.

* If you are in the Print Preview, click the **Setup** button. Otherwise, use the **File - Page Setup** command.

* If necessary, activate the **Header/Footer** tab.

*You can also use the **View - Header and Footer** command.*

* If you wish, you can select a pre-set **Header** and/or **Footer** from the corresponding list.

Headers and footers chosen from the list are automatically centred at the top/bottom of the page.

* If you want to create your own header and footer:

  - click the **Custom Header** and/or **Custom Footer** button.

  - activate the text box that corresponds to the required position on the page (**Left section, Center section, Right section**).

  - enter the text to be printed.

* To create a second (or third…) line of text, use the ↵ key.

▪ To insert variable details, click the appropriate buttons:

Page number	
Total number of pages	
Date of printing	
Time of printing	
Workbook name and file path	
Name of workbook	
Name of worksheet	
Picture	

Header [?] [X]

To format text: select the text, then choose the font button.
To insert a page number, date, time, file path, filename, or tab name: position the
   insertion point in the edit box, then choose the appropriate button.
To insert picture: press the Insert Picture button. To format your picture, place the
   cursor in the edit box and press the Format Picture button.

OK
Cancel

A [#] [#] [#] [#] [#] [#] [#] [#] [#]

Left section: Center section: Right section:

| My Project | | &[Date] |

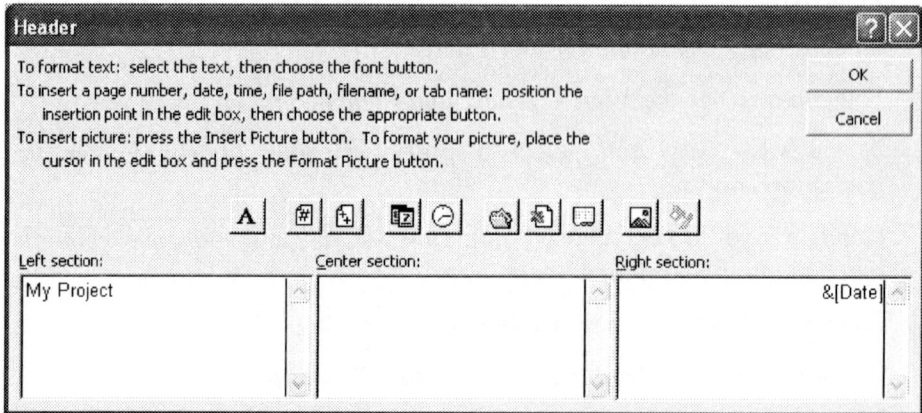

Each of these variables corresponds to a code which appears between square brackets.

▪ If you wish, you can format the text or variable you have entered by selecting it and clicking the **A** button.

▪ Click **OK**.

Excel displays a preview of the header and footer as it will look in print.

» When you have defined your header and footer, click **OK**.

3 ▪ Repeating titles on each page

Certain rows and/or columns (containing headings for example) can be repeated on each printed page.

» **File - Page Setup**

» If necessary, activate the **Sheet** tab.

» Activate the **Rows to repeat at top** box and/or the **Columns to repeat at left** box.

» Click the ▦ button to collapse the dialog box then, on the worksheet, select a cell in the row(s) and/or column(s) which you want to repeat.

	A	B	C	D	E	
1						
2		Page Setup - Rows to repeat at top:				? ✕
3		$4:$4				▦
4	Surname	First Name	Address	PC/City	Sex	Occu
5	Stoner	Carla	56 Lawrence St	4000 Westport	F	Librarian
6	Barton	John	37 Chambers St	4000 Westport	M	Teacher

In this example, row 4 containing the titles concerning the names, addresses and so on will appear on each page printed.

» Click ▦ to expand the dialog box again.

» Click **OK**.

Exercise 6.2: Page Setup

Below, you can see **Practice Exercise** 6.2. This exercise is made up of 3 steps. If you do not know how to do one of the steps, go back to the title that corresponds to that particular lesson. When you have finished, you can check your work by reading the **Solution** that follows.

All the steps in this exercise are likely to be tested in the MOUS exam.

☞ Practice Exercise 6.2

---

*To work on exercise 6.2, you should open the **6-2 Furniture.xls** workbook located in the **MOUS Excel 2002** folder.*

1. For **Sheet1**, make the page setup changes described below:

   - apply a **Landscape** orientation to the page,

   - ensure that cell gridlines and row and column headers appear during printing,

   - change the top margin of **Sheet1** to **3.5**.

2. Insert the date in the right section of the header and the page number in the centre section of the footer.

3. Repeat the headings on row **4** on each printed page.

If you want to put what you have learnt into practice on a real document, you can work on summary exercise 6 for the PRINTING section that you can find at the end of this book.

It is often possible to perform a task in several different ways, but here, only the easiest solution is presented. You can go back to the corresponding lesson if you want to see other techniques you could use.

Solution to Exercise 6.2

1. To change the page setup for Sheet1 of the 6-2 Furniture.xls workbook, click the **Sheet1** tab if necessary then use the **File - Page Setup** command.

   To apply a Landscape orientation to the page, click the **Page** tab on the **Page Setup** dialog box then, in the **Orientation** frame, activate the **Landscape** option.

   To ensure that cell gridlines and row and column headers appear during printing, click the **Sheet** tab on the **Page Setup** dialog box then tick the **Gridlines** and **Row and column headings** check boxes.

   To change the top margin of Sheet1 to 3.5, click the **Margins** tab. Click the **Top** text box and enter **3.5**.

   Click **OK** to confirm the changes made to the page setup.

2. To insert the date in the right section of the header and the page number in the centre section of the footer, use the **File - Page Setup** command then click the **Header/Footer** tab.
   Click the **Custom Header** button then click the **Right section** box.
   Click the 🗓 tool button then click **OK**.
   Click the **Custom Footer** button then click the **Center section** box.
   Click the # tool button then click **OK**.
   Click **OK** to confirm the changes made to the **Page Setup** dialog box.

3. To repeat the headings in row 4 on each printed page, use the **File - Page Setup** command then click the **Sheet** tab.

   Click the ▣ button in the **Rows to repeat at top** box then click cell **A4** on the worksheet.

   Click the ▣ button then click **OK**.

DRAWING OBJECTS
Lesson 7.1: Charts

1▪ Creating a chart in a worksheet.. 204

2▪ Defining page setup for a chart.. 207

3▪ Previewing a chart before printing 208

4▪ Printing a chart.. 209

5▪ Activating/deactivating an embedded chart 209

6▪ Selecting the different objects in a chart 210

7▪ Changing chart type 212

8▪ Inserting gridlines in a chart 213

9▪ Modifying the display of tick marks and tick mark labels 214

10▪Managing a chart legend 215

11▪Deleting a data series 215

12▪Adding a data series to an embedded chart... 216

13▪Adding/deleting a data category 217

Practice Exercise 7.1 219

DRAWING OBJECTS
Lesson 7.1: Charts

🗒1 ▪ Creating a chart in a worksheet

▪ If the data needed for the chart is contained in a continuous block of cells, select that range.

▪ If the data for the chart is in several different ranges, select the nonadjacent ranges in the usual way (with Ctrl-clicks). So Excel can analyse the data correctly, make sure the cell ranges selected form a coherent set each time, including blank cells if necessary.

	A	B	C	D	
1		JANUARY	FEBRUARY	MARCH	
2	PETER	4,568.90	3,958.00	4,578.50	Excel considers
3	CALLUM	2,587.00	3,250.00	2,356.00	the selected
4	SUE	6,589.10	3,845.00	4,578.90	ranges as one
5	JOSH	6,348.00	7,890.00	7,845.10	rectangular block
6	ANNE	2,890.00	4,560.00	3,589.00	
7	WENDY	4,578.90	7,125.00	4,560.00	
8	BEN	3,875.00	4,500.00	5,230.00	
9	PHILIP	4,580.00	5,845.00	2,356.00	

A	C
	FEBRUARY
PETER	3,958.00
CALLUM	3,250.00
ANNE	4,560.00
WENDY	7,125.00

In the example above, the blank cell in the top left corner was included to ensure a symmetrical selection was made.

▪ **Insert - Chart** or 📊

▪ Select the **Chart type** then the **Chart sub-type**.

▪ Click the **Next** button.

▪ Check the references of the selected cells in the **Data range** box and if necessary, modify the selection using the 🔲 button. Indicate whether the series are in rows or columns (**Rows** or **Columns** option).
If the chart shown does not resemble the required chart, click the **Series** tab to check the references of each series. To do that, select a **Series** in the list then check, and modify if required, its **Name** and the **Values** of the cells that make up that series. You can also verify, and change, the **Category (X) axis labels**.

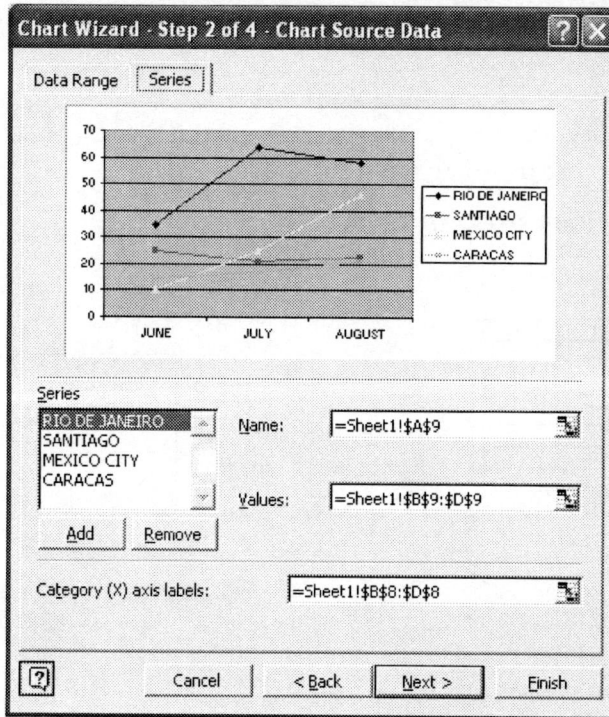

Chart Wizard - Step 2 of 4 - Chart Source Data

Data Range | Series

Series
RIO DE JANEIRO
SANTIAGO
MEXICO CITY
CARACAS

Name: =Sheet1!$A$9

Values: =Sheet1!$B$9:$D$9

Add | Remove

Category (X) axis labels: =Sheet1!$B$8:$D$8

Cancel | < Back | Next > | Finish

» Click **Next**.

» Customise your chart by giving the various chart titles on the **Titles** page. At this stage in the wizard, you can also select options from the other tabs (cf. below).

» Click **Next**.

» To create the chart on a separate chart sheet, activate the **As new sheet** option and give the name of the sheet you are creating. Otherwise, leave the **As object in** option active and select the sheet in which to insert the chart.

» Click **Finish**.

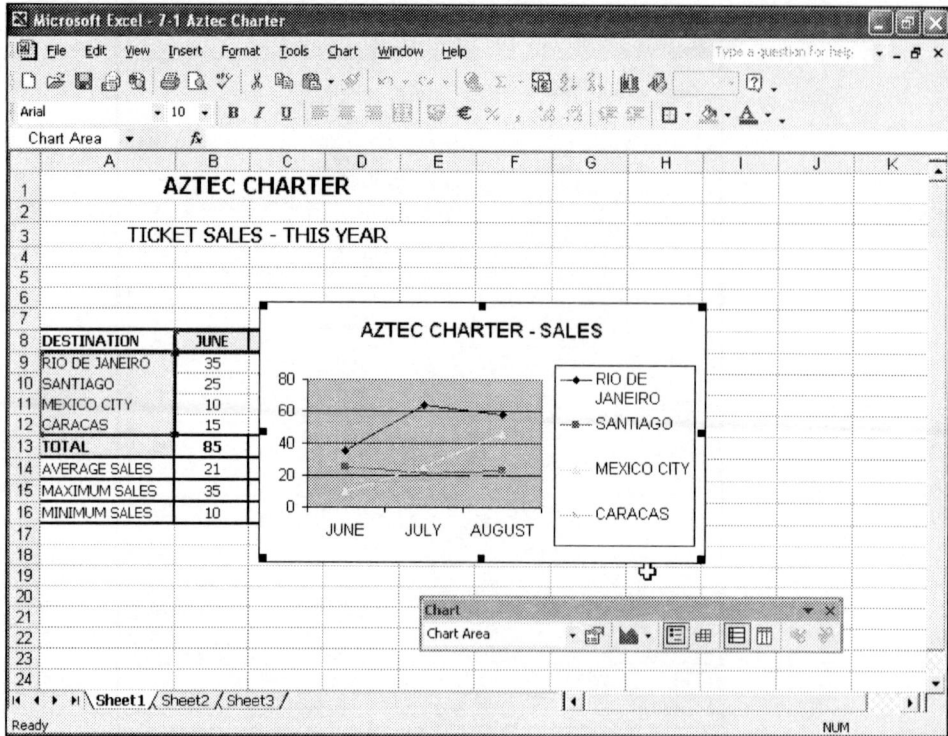

On the example above, the chart has been inserted as an object in the active worksheet.

When you insert a chart as an object in the active sheet, it appears in the workspace. It is surrounded by black squares (handles) to show it is selected. This type of chart is an **embedded chart**.

When you select an embedded chart made from data adjacent to it on the worksheet, coloured rectangles appear around certain cell ranges. These highlight the data on the sheet that is used in the chart:

- data series are enclosed in a green rectangle,

- categories are enclosed in a purple rectangle,

- data points are enclosed in a blue rectangle.

* If necessary, move the chart as you would move any other drawing object: point to one of its edges and drag it. You can also resize a chart by dragging one of its handles.

In a 2D chart, each series can contain up to 32002 points and in a 3D chart, up to 4000.

Unless you alter the default, a chart and its source data are linked and any changes to the data are carried over into the chart.

2 ▪ Defining page setup for a chart

* Select the chart.

* If you are in Print Preview, click the **Setup** button. Otherwise, use the **File - Page Setup** command.

*The usual options on offer when printing worksheets are not all available when you are working with a chart. The **Sheet** tab disappears but a new tab called **Chart** replaces it.*

* In addition to the normal page setup options, you can also adjust the **Printed chart size** under the **Chart** tab:

Use full page   distorts the proportions of the chart so that it fills the whole page.

Scale to fit page   increase the size of the chart as much as the page allows, without distorting its proportions.

Custom   prints a chart the same size as the chart on the screen.

* Click **OK**.

⊞3 ▪ Previewing a chart before printing

▪ Select the chart if you want to preview only the chart: if you want to preview it along with the other data on the worksheet, click outside the chart.

▪ **File - Print Preview** or

A scaled-down image of the sheet appears, as it will look when printed.

▪ To zoom in on the preview, position the pointer over the area you want to magnify and click, or click the **Zoom** button.

Before you click, the pointer takes the shape of a magnifying glass; once you are in zoom mode, it becomes an arrow.

▪ To return to the scaled-down sheet, click the page again or click the **Zoom** button.

▪ To display another page, use the **Next** and **Previous** buttons. When in the scaled-down version of the document, you can also use the vertical scroll bar to change page.

▪ To change the margins and column widths, click the **Margins** button.

▪ To manage page breaks on the active page, click the **Page Break Preview** button.

▪ To leave the Print Preview, click the **Close** button or press Esc on the keyboard.

📖4 ▪ Printing a chart

※ Select the chart.

If you do not select the chart, any other information on the worksheet will be printed along with it.

※ **File - Print** or ⌨ Ctrl **P**

※ Under **Print range**, activate the **All** option to print all the pages of the worksheet. If you want to print a certain number of pages, click the **From** box and enter the number of the first page to be printed then click the **To** box and enter the number of the last page you want to print.

※ Leave the **Selected Chart** option active in the **Print what** frame.

*In the **Print what** frame, the normal options available for worksheets (**Selection, Entire workbook**) are unavailable because the chart is selected.*

※ In the **Number of copies** box, specify how many copies you wish to print.

※ The **Collate** option prints a document as several entire copies, instead of multiple copies of each page: if you do not want the document collated in this way, deactivate the **Collate** option.

※ Click **OK** to start printing.

📖5 ▪ Activating/deactivating an embedded chart

※ To activate an embedded chart, click it once to select the whole chart object then if necessary click to select one of the chart items.

*The **Chart** menu replaces the **Data** menu.*

※ To deactivate an embedded chart, click a cell in the sheet, outside the chart.

※ To display an embedded chart in a separate window, select it then use **View - Chart Window**. Close this window to deactivate the chart.

6 • Selecting the different objects in a chart

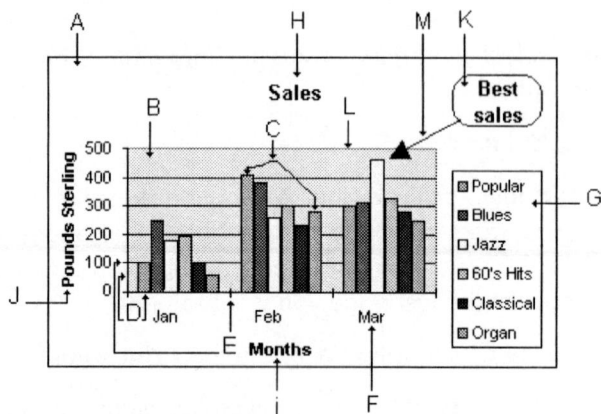

	Object	How to select it	What it contains
A	Chart area	Click in the chart but not in any object	All the chart objects
B	Plot area	Click in the plot area but not in any object	The axes and data markers
C	Point	Click the series then click the point	Each value in a series
	Series	Click one of the data markers in the series	All the points that constitute a data series
D	Value axis / Category axis	Click one of the tick mark labels	
E	Tick marks	No selection	Lines which divide up the axes

	Object	How to select it	What it contains
F	Tick mark labels	No selection	Texts attached to tick marks
G	Legend	Click the object	Shows the names of the series represented in the chart and identifies the symbol or colour used for the data markers
H	Chart title	Click the object	Attached text
I	Value axis title	Click the object	Attached text
J	Category axis title	Click the object	Attached text
K	Text box	Click the object	Unttached text
L	Gridlines	Click one of the lines	Lines crossing the plot area to make it easier to read the chart
M	Arrow	Click the object	

*When you point to an object in a chart, its name and value appears in a ScreenTip, providing that the **Show names** and **Show values** options are active in the **Options** dialog box, **Chart** tab (**Tools - Options**). You can also select a chart object by opening the list box on the **Chart** toolbar (**View - Toolbars - Chart**) and clicking the object's name.*

*To access a dialog box in which you can format a chart object, select the object then use the first command in the **Format** menu. This command name changes depending on the object. You can also double-click the item you wish to modify.*

⊞7 ▪ Changing chart type

* If you want to change the chart type for all the data series in the chart, select the entire chart (the square black handles that appear around the edge of the chart show that it has been selected).
  If you want to change the chart type for just one of the series, select the series in question.

* **Chart - Chart Type**

* Choose the **Chart type**.

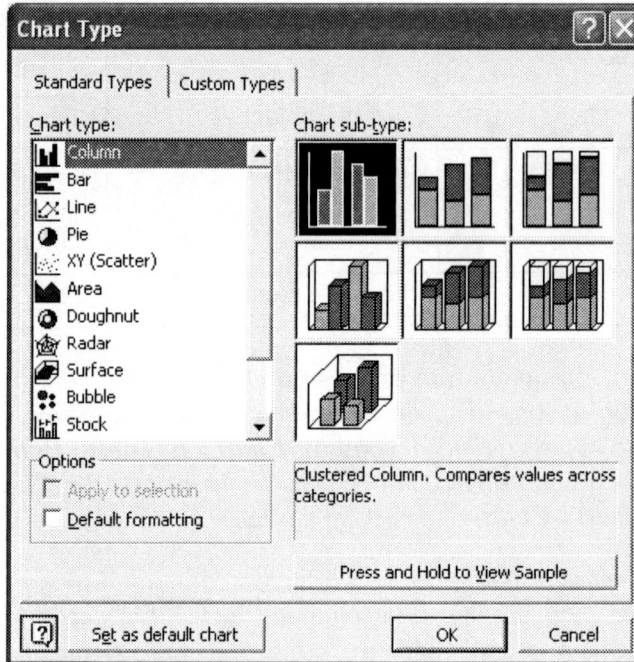

The **Apply to selection** option is not available when you are changing the chart type of the whole chart.

* Double-click the **Chart sub-type** of your choice.

The ▲▾ button on the **Chart** toolbar can be used to change chart type but does not allow you to choose between the various sub-types.

The **Source Data** option in the **Chart** menu allows you to redefine the different series in the chart.

All the options for managing the chart can be found in **Chart - Chart Options**.

8 ▪ Inserting gridlines in a chart

▪ Select the chart.

▪ **Chart - Chart Options - Gridlines** tab

▪ Activate the options in the **Category (X) axis** frame to add vertical gridlines to the chart.

▪ Activate the options in the **Value (Y) axis** frame to add horizontal gridlines to the chart.

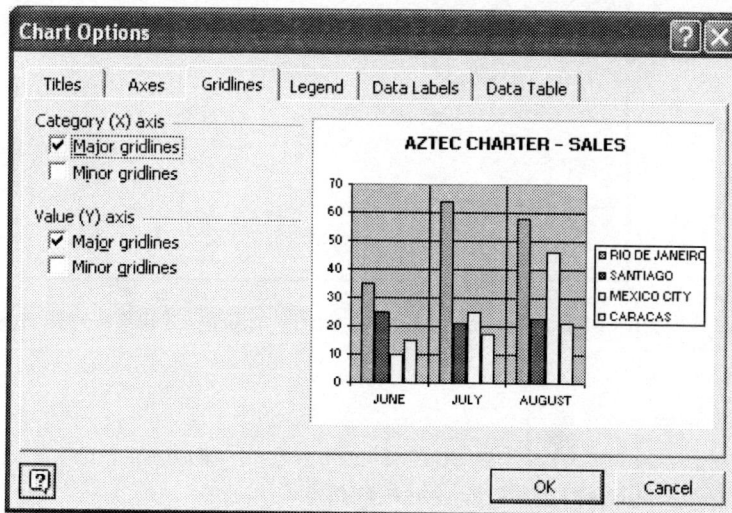

- Click **OK**.

📖9 ▪ Modifying the display of tick marks and tick mark labels

- Select the category axis whose tick marks and/or tick mark labels need formatting.

- **Format - Selected Axis** or ⬜ or ⌨ **1**

- Use the **Font** and **Number** tabs to define the format of text and numbers in the labels.

- Define the position of the tick marks and the labels relative to the axis, using the options under the **Patterns** tab:

Format Axis

Tabs: Patterns | Scale | Font | Number | Alignment

Lines
- Automatic
- None
- Custom

Style: _____
Color: Automatic
Weight: _____

Sample

Major tick mark type
- None • Outside
- Inside Cross

Minor tick mark type
- • None Outside
- Inside Cross

Tick mark labels
- None High
- Low • Next to axis

OK   Cancel

- On the **Alignment** page, determine the orientation of the text in the labels.

- Click **OK**.

📄 The ⬜ and ⬜ tool buttons on the **Chart** toolbar can be used to change the orientation of the text in the labels.

10 ▪ Managing a chart legend

- If necessary, activate the chart.
- **Chart - Chart Options - Legend** tab
- Choose whether or not to **Show legend** by ticking or deactivating the check box.
- In the **Placement** frame, choose the required position for the legend.
- Click **OK**.

📄 The legend is displayed horizontally when moved to the top or the bottom of the chart.

Click the ▦ tool button on the **Chart** toolbar to display or hide the legend.

🖲 The legend can also be dragged to its new position.

11 ▪ Deleting a data series

- Select the chart.
- **Chart - Source Data - Series** tab
- In the **Series** list, select the series you want to delete.
- Click the **Remove** button.
- Click **OK**.

🖲 You can also delete a data series by clicking it in the chart then pressing the `Del` key.

▦12 ▪ Adding a data series to an embedded chart

First method

This can be used only when the series to be added is next to a series already included in the chart.

▪ Select the chart area.

On the worksheet, the cells containing the data series are enclosed in a green rectangle.

▪ Drag the handle of the green rectangle until it has encompassed the values of the new series (make sure the pointer looks like a double-headed, and not a four-headed, arrow).

Second method

▪ Select the cells containing the values corresponding to the series.

▪ Drag the selection onto the chart.

📄 *This method is very quick but can be used only for embedded charts when the source data is close by. If the chart is in a chart sheet, you can copy the source data using the clipboard.*

Third method

▪ **Chart - Source Data - Series** tab

▪ Click the **Add** button.

Excel creates a new series called Series1.

▪ Click the **Name** box and give the new series a name.

- Click the **Values** box and click the 🔲 button to work in the sheet. Select the cells containing the values for the new series and click 🔲 to restore the dialog box.
- Click **OK**.

  📄 *This command can also be used to change the cells associated with a series.*

  *You can also use the **Chart - Add Data** command.*

  If you wish to add a series or category to a chart sheet, you must select and copy (📑) the cells corresponding to the series or category then paste (📋) them into the chart sheet.

13 ▪ Adding/deleting a data category

Either the mouse or the menus can be used to add or delete a category in an embedded chart.

- Select the chart area.
- To add a new category, and its corresponding data points, drag the handle of the purple rectangle until it encompasses the cells containing the new category. To delete a category, reduce the rectangle so the data in question is excluded from it.

  📄 *This method can be used only in the case of an embedded chart, with the source data close by.*

  If the category you wish to add is not adjacent to the existing categories, you can select the corresponding cells and drag them into the chart.

DRAWING OBJECTS
Lesson 7.1: Charts

- Select the chart area.

- **Chart - Add Data**

- In the **Range** text box, give the references of the data you want to add then click **OK**.

  The *Paste Special* dialog box may appear.

- If this occurs, activate the **New point(s)** option. In the **Values (Y) in** frame, indicate whether the series are in rows or columns. Activate the **Categories (X Labels) in First Column** (or **Row**) option if the selected range contains category labels.

- Click **OK**.

Below, you can see **Practice Exercise** 7.1. This exercise is made up of 13 steps. If you do not know how to do one of the steps, go back to the title that corresponds to that particular lesson. When you have finished, you can check your work by reading the **Solution** that follows.

All the steps in this exercise are likely to be tested in the MOUS exam.

☞ Practice Exercise 7.1

*To work on exercise 7.1, you should open the **7-1 Aztec Charter.xls** workbook in the **MOUS Excel 2002** folder then activate **Sheet1**.*

1. Insert the following chart under the table in worksheet **Sheet1**:

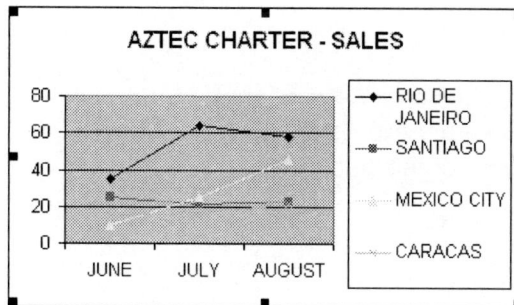

2. Modify the chart's page setup so its size is adjusted to the page when printed.

3. Preview the chart as it would appear when printed, then close the Print Preview.

4. Print two copies of the chart.

5. Display the chart in its own window, then close that window.

6. Select the chart title.

7. Change the chart type to a clustered column.

8. Add major gridlines to the value and category axes.

9. Change the font size of the category axis tick mark labels to **6 points**.

10. Display the legend below the chart.

11. Delete the **Caracas** series from the chart.

12. Add the **Caracas** series to the chart again.

13. Delete the **August** data category from the chart.

If you want to put what you have learnt into practice on a real document, you can work on summary exercise 7 for the DRAWING OBJECTS section that you can find at the end of this book.

It is often possible to perform a task in several different ways, but here, only the easiest solution is presented. You can go back to the corresponding lesson if you want to see other techniques you could use.

Solution to Exercise 7.1

1. To insert the chart, select cells **A8:D12** then use the **Insert - Chart** command.
   Click the **Line** chart type then click the first sub-type in the second row. Click the **Next** button.

   In **Data range**, check that the cell range reference is **=Sheet1!$A$8:$D$12** then activate the **Rows** option. Click the **Next** button to go to the next step. If necessary, click the **Titles** tab.
   Enter **AZTEC CHARTER - SALES** in the **Chart title** box and click **Next**.
   In the **As object in** box, leave **Sheet1** selected. Click the **Finish** button.

   Drag the chart underneath the table.

2. To make the chart adjust to one page when printed, click the chart to select it, use the **File - Page Setup** command and click the **Chart** tab.
   Click the **Scale to fit page** option under **Printed chart size** then click **OK**.

3. To preview the chart, select it then click the 🔍 tool button.
   Once you have viewed the chart, click the **Close** button to leave the Print Preview.

4. To print two copies of the chart, click the chart to select it then use the **File - Print** command.
   Enter **2** in the **Number of copies** box then click **OK** to start printing.

5. To show the chart in a separate window, click the chart to select it, then use the **View - Chart Window** command. To close the chart window, click the ☒ button on its title bar.

6. To select the chart title, click the **AZTEC CHARTER - SALES** text.

7. To change the chart type to a clustered column, click the chart to select it then use the **Chart - Chart Type** command.
Select **Column** as the **Chart type** then choose the first **Chart sub-type** offered.
Click **OK**.

8. To add major gridlines to the value axis and the category axis, click the chart to select it, use the **Chart - Chart Options** command then click the **Gridlines** tab.
Activate the **Major gridlines** option in both the **Category (X) axis** and **Value (Y) axis** frames then click **OK**.

9. To change the font size to 6 on the category axis tick mark labels, click one of the tick mark labels on the Category axis (June, for example), use **Format - Selected Axis** then click the **Font** tab.
Select the value in the **Size** box and enter **6** then click **OK**.

10. To display the legend under the chart, double-click the legend then click the **Placement** tab.
Activate the **Bottom** option then click **OK**.

11. To delete the **Caracas** series from the chart, click the chart to select it, use **Chart - Source Data** then click the **Series** tab.
Select **Caracas** in the **Series** list, click the **Remove** button then **OK**.

12. To add the **Caracas** series back into the chart, select the chart area. In the table on the worksheet, drag the green selection handle you can see at the bottom right of cell **D11** down to cell **D12**.

13. To delete the **August** data category from the chart, select the chart area. Drag the blue selection handle you can see at the bottom right of cell **D12** across to the right, over cell **C12**.

DRAWING OBJECTS
Lesson 7.2: Drawing objects

1 ▪ Creating a drawing object 224

2 ▪ Creating a text box... 226

3 ▪ Inserting a picture, sound or video 227

4 ▪ Resizing/moving an object... 233

5 ▪ Selecting objects... 234

6 ▪ Changing an object's appearance 234

7 ▪ Deleting objects 235

Practice Exercise 7.2 236

DRAWING OBJECTS
Lesson 7.2: Drawing objects

🖻 1 ▪ Creating a drawing object

Drawing an object

- Display the **Drawing** toolbar by clicking the ⬚ tool button.

- Click the button that corresponds to the shape you wish to draw or click the **AutoShapes** button and choose one of the shapes given in the sub-menus.

- Drag to draw the shape on the workspace. Hold down the ⬚Alt key as you drag to align the object to the cell grid.

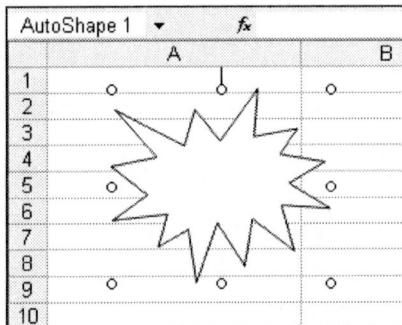

The name of the object drawn appears on the left of the formula bar.

📄 *Hold down the ⬚Shift key when you draw if you wish to make an evenly-proportioned square, circle or arc, or a perfectly horizontal, vertical or diagonal line.*

Inserting a WordArt object

The WordArt application is used to apply special effects to text:

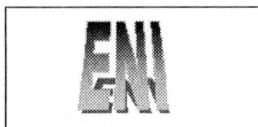

- Click the ▣ tool button in the **Drawing** toolbar.

- Select an effect then click **OK**.

- Type the text to which you want to apply the WordArt effect; use the ⏎ key when you want to create a line break.

- Use the **Font** and **Font Size** lists as well as the ▣ and ▣ tool buttons to format the text.

- Click **OK**.

The text appears on the worksheet as a drawing object.

📄 *When a WordArt text object is selected, you can edit it using the tools from the **WordArt** toolbar.*

Inserting a diagram

Here is an example of an organization chart type of diagram:

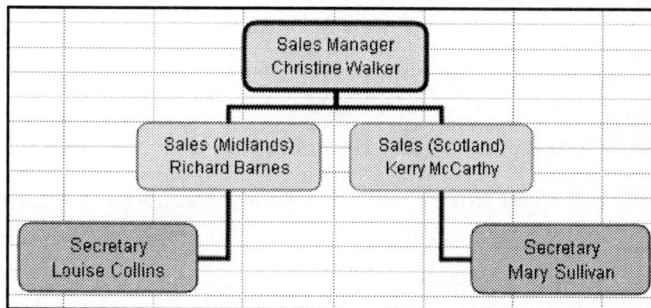

- Click the ▣ tool button on the **Drawing** toolbar.

- Select the type of diagram you wish to use then click **OK**.

*The chosen type of diagram appears in a drawing canvas and the **Organization Chart** toolbar appears (if you choose that type of diagram): if you choose another type, the **Diagram** toolbar appears.*

* Enter your text in the **Click to add text** boxes. When you have filled in all the required text, click outside the diagram to end text entry.

* To add another shape to an **Organization Chart**, choose the shape to which you wish to add a new one then open the **Insert Shape** list on the **Organization Chart** toolbar and select the type of shape you wish to add. For other types of diagram, just click the **Insert Shape** button on the **Diagram** toolbar.

* To delete a shape from a diagram, click the edge of the shape to select it, then press [Del].

*The [icon] tool button on the **Organization Chart** or **Diagram** toolbar applies an automatic format to the diagram.*

To delete a diagram, click it to activate it then click its hatched border and press [Del].

2 ▪ Creating a text box

A text box is a drawing object that is designed to contain text.

* Click the [icon] tool button on the **Drawing** toolbar.

* Drag to draw the text box or click the place you wish to start entering the text. Use the [Alt] key as you drag if you wish to align the text box to the cell grid.

Once the text box has been created, an insertion point appears inside it.

* Enter your text, without worrying about line breaks. Use the [↵] key when you want to start a new paragraph.

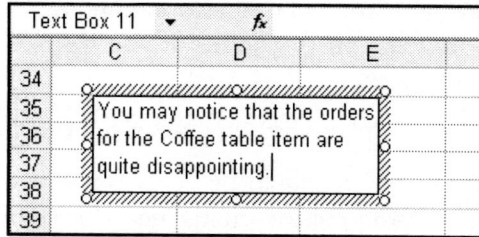

Text Box 11 ▼		f_x	
	C	D	E
34			
35	You may notice that the orders		
36	for the Coffee table item are		
37	quite disappointing.|		
38			
39			

- If necessary, format the characters entered.

- Press ⎋Esc when you have finished your text.

   *To add text to a drawing or AutoShape, right-click the drawn shape and select **Add Text**.*

▥ 3 ▪ Inserting a picture, sound or video

Finding and inserting a picture, a sound or a video clip

- If necessary, use the **Insert - Picture - Clip Art** command to display the **Insert Clip Art** task pane.

*The **Add Clips to Organizer** dialog box may appear on the screen:*

Add Clips to Organizer

Welcome to Microsoft Clip Organizer!

Clip Organizer can catalog picture, sound, and motion files found on your hard disk(s) or in folders you specify.

Click Now to catalog all media files. Click Later to postpone this task. Click Options to specify folders.

☐ Don't show this message again

[Now] [Later] [Options...]

- Click the **Now** button if you want to add the image, audio and video files from your hard disk into the Clip Organizer. If you do not want to do that just yet, click the **Later** button.

- Enter one or more search keywords in the **Search text** box in the task pane.

- To define where the search should be carried out, open the **Search in** list and make a choice, following these guidelines: the plus (+) sign expands the hierarchy while the minus (-) sign collapses it. Click a check box once to select the corresponding category: click twice to select that category and all its subcategories. Click a third time to deselect that category but keep the selected subcategories selected and click a fourth time to deselect all the subcategories.

*The **Office Collections** category and its subcategories correspond to the image, sound and video elements installed with Office. The **Web Collections** category provides you with elements found on the Web (or more precisely on the Microsoft site). Excel will take this category into account only if you have an open Internet connection.*

- To limit the type of items being searched for (**Clip Art, Photographs, Movies** or **Sounds**), open the **Results should be** list and deselect any elements that should be excluded from the search. You can also limit the search to certain file types. To do this, click the plus (+) sign on the type of element concerned and deselect any file types that should not be included in the search.

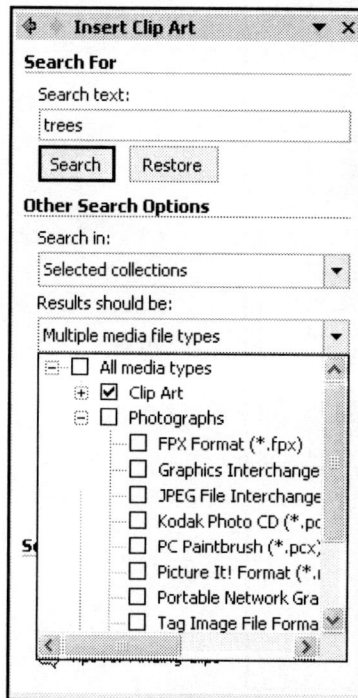

* Click the **Search** button.

*If you want to interrupt the search, click the **Stop** button that appears near the bottom of the pane.*

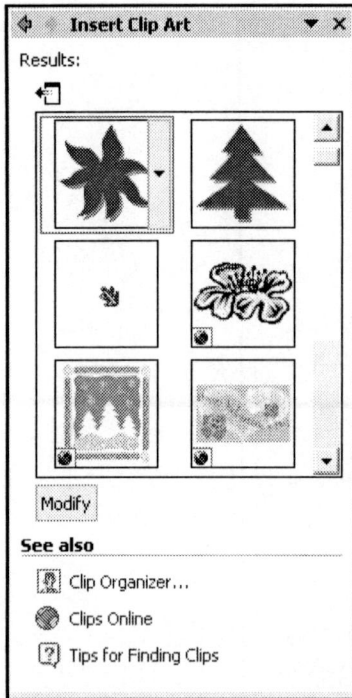

If the [icon] icon appears at the bottom left of an item, this indicates it was found on the Web. This will occur only if you have included the Web as one of your search areas and your Internet connection is open.

- When the search is finished or if you click the **Stop** button, the **Modify** button appears, which you can use to set up a new search.

- To insert one of the items found into your active document, select the cell where you wish to put the item then click the clip in the **Insert Clip Art** task pane.

- To see options relating to the image, point to it, then click the bar with the arrow that appears on the right side of the clip.

Insert

Copy

Delete from Clip Organizer

Open Clip In... ← opens the image
                  in another
Tools on the Web...   application

Copy to Collection...

Move to Collection...

Edit Keywords... ← use to modify
                    the keywords
Find Similar Style   associated with
                      the image
Preview/Properties

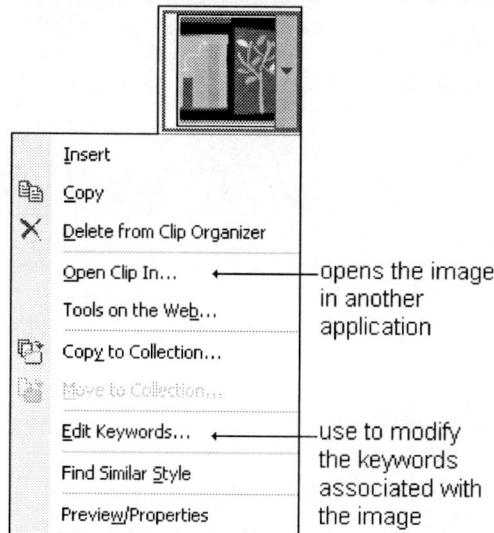

■ If necessary, close the task pane by clicking its [X] button.

The Clips Online link at the bottom of the Insert Clip Art task pane takes you to the Microsoft site where you can make your own search.

Using the Clip Organizer

■ If necessary, use the **Insert - Picture - Clip Art** command to display the **Insert Clip Art** task pane.

The Add Clips to Organizer dialog box may appear on the screen: click the Now button if you want to add the image, audio and video files from your hard disk into the Clip Organizer. If you do not want to do that just yet, click the Later button.

■ Click the **Clip Organizer** link at the bottom of the task pane.

■ To browse the collections of image, sound or video items available in Office, expand the **Office Collections** hierarchy (click the + sign) then click the subcategory of your choice to display its contents in the right half of the window.

DRAWING OBJECTS
Lesson 7.2: Drawing objects

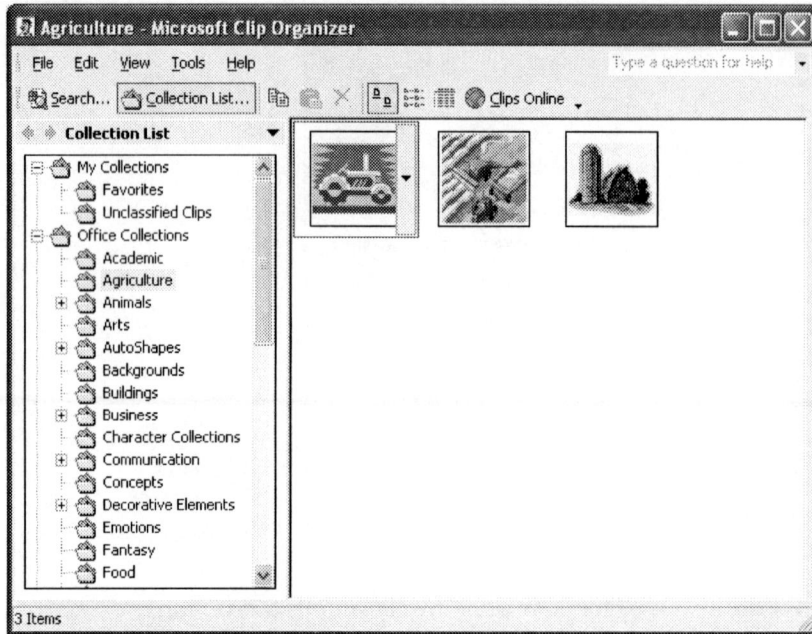

* In the **My Collections** collection, you can create and manage your own custom subcollections:

  - To create a new collection within **My Collections**, select **My Collections** then use the **File - New Collection** command and enter the new collection's **Name**. Decide where to store this new collection then click **OK**.

  - To copy a picture, sound or video clip into a subcollection of **My Collections**, look for the item in the **Office Collections** or **Web Collections** (if you are connected to the Internet) then drag the item from the right pane into the required subcollection in the left pane.

  *If you point to a clip in the right pane of the **Clip Organizer** window, a bar with an arrow appears on the clip; this contains the same menu of options described above.*

* You can also add a picture, sound or video clip to your document by dragging the item from the right pane of the **Clip Organizer** window onto the active document.

  *The **Clip Organizer** window disappears but is still open in the background; you can reactivate it by clicking its button on the taskbar.*

* Close the **Clip Organizer** by clicking the ▣ button on its window then, if necessary, close the **Insert Clip Art** task pane.

  📄 *To see more complex AutoShapes in the **Insert Clip Art** task pane, click the **AutoShapes** button on the **Drawing** toolbar and choose the **More AutoShapes** option.*

  *To tile a picture over the background of the active sheet, activate the sheet, use **Format - Sheet - Background**, search for the image using the dialog box then click the **Insert** button.*

  *To resize the selected picture, use **Format - Picture - Size** tab, then enter a new **Height** and **Width** in the **Size and rotate** frame.*

4 ▪ Resizing/moving an object

* Select the drawing object concerned.

  *The small circles surrounding the selected object are called **handles**. The white circles are used to resize the object, while the green circle can rotate the object. When you place the mouse pointer over each type of handle, the pointer changes shape.*

* To resize an object, drag one of the selection handles. If you drag a corner handle, the object's proportions are unaffected.

  *The current size of the object, as a percentage of its original size can be seen in the **Name Box** on the left of the formula bar.*

* To rotate an object, point to the green circle at the top of the object and drag it to make the rotation.

* To move an object, drag the object into its new position.

📄 *Use the* ⌗Alt⌗ *key as you drag to align the object with the cell grid.*

5 ▪ Selecting objects

▪ Click the 🔲 tool button on the **Drawing** toolbar.

▪ Click an object to select it.

▪ To select several objects, hold down the ⌗Shift⌗ key and click each object to select it.

📄 *When several objects are selected, no name appears on the formula bar.*

🔍 *You can also select several objects by dragging an invisible rectangle around them.*

6 ▪ Changing an object's appearance

A 2D object

▪ Select the object.

▪ Use the tool buttons on the **Drawing** toolbar:

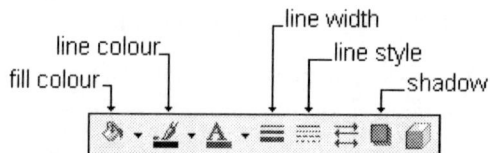

The ⌗ *tool button is used to define arrowheads for line objects.*

*To remove an object's borders, select it then choose **Format - Text Box** or **Picture - Colors and Lines** tab. Go into the **Color** list and choose the **No Line** option.*

A 3D object

» Select the object then click the ⬛ tool button on the **Drawing** toolbar to select a pre-set 3D style. If none of these styles is suitable, click the **3D Settings** button to create a specific 3D effect:

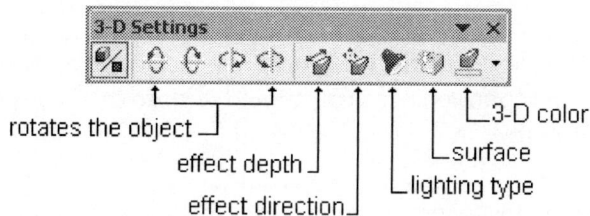

*Some of these effects can be found in the **Format** dialog box: double-click the object to display this dialog box.*

▦7 ▪ Deleting objects

» Select the object(s) that you wish to delete.
» Press the ⌷Del⌷ key on the keyboard.

Below, you can see **Practice Exercise** 7.2. This exercise is made up of 7 steps. If you do not know how to do one of the steps, go back to the title that corresponds to that particular lesson. When you have finished, you can check your work by reading the **Solution** that follows.

Steps that are likely to be tested during the MOUS exam are marked with this symbol: 🔳. However, it is a good idea to complete the whole exercise to ensure you have understood everything covered in the lesson.

☞ **Practice Exercise 7.2**

To work on exercise 7.2, you should open the **7-2 Furniture.xls** workbook in the **MOUS Excel 2002** folder then activate **Sheet1**.

🔳 1. Insert the text **Furniture World** as a WordArt object, placing the two words on separate lines. You should choose the Word Art effect located on the fourth row, in the fourth column (for now, do not move the object).

🔳 2. Create the following text box, under the table (around cell C34):

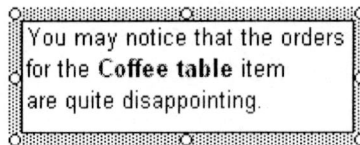

You may notice that the orders
for the **Coffee table** item
are quite disappointing.

Remember to put the words Coffee table in bold type.

3. Using the **Insert Clip Art** task pane, look for pictures in the **Office Collections** concerning **trees**. Insert into the worksheet the first picture in the list of pictures found.

Close the **Insert Clip Art** task pane.

4. Resize the picture of the tree keeping its proportions until it is 70% of its original size then move it towards cell **E2**.
Next, move the Furniture World WordArt object up so the table's title can be seen again.

5. Select the WordArt object (Furniture World) and the picture (the tree), then deselect them.

6. Apply a yellow colour to the outline of the WordArt text (Furniture World), black to the text box border and red to the text within the text box.

7. Delete the picture of the tree.

If you want to put what you have learnt into practice on a real document, you can work on summary exercise 7 for the DRAWING OBJECTS section that you can find at the end of this book.

It is often possible to perform a task in several different ways, but here, only the easiest solution is presented. You can go back to the corresponding lesson if you want to see other techniques you could use.

Solution to Exercise 7.2

1. To insert the text «Furniture World» as a WordArt object, click the ![tool] tool button on the **Drawing** toolbar then choose the fourth WordArt effect on the fourth row and click **OK**.
Type **Furniture**, press ⏎ on the keyboard, type **World** then click **OK**.

   You will move the WordArt object later in the exercise.

2. To create a text box, click the ![tool] tool button. Click cell **C34**, type the text **You may notice that the orders**, press ⏎, type **for the Coffee table item**, press ⏎ then type **are quite disappointing**.

   Select the words **Coffee table**, click the **B** tool button then press Esc on the keyboard.

3. To use the Insert Clip Art task pane to look for pictures in the Office Collections concerning trees, use the **Insert - Picture - Clip Art** command to display the **Insert Clip Art** task pane.
If the **Add Clips to Organizer** dialog box appears on the screen, click the **Now** button if you want to add the image, audio and video files from your hard disk into the Clip Organizer now or the **Later** button if you do not want to do that.
Enter the keyword **trees** into the **Search text** box.

Open the **Search in** list and make sure that only the **Office Collections** folder is chosen.

Open the **Results should be** list and make sure that only the **Clip Art** category is active.

Click the **Search** button to start the search.

To insert the first picture from the list of images found into the worksheet, drag the clip from the task pane into **Sheet1**.

To close the **Insert Clip Art** task pane, click the ☒ button at the top right of the pane.

4. To resize the picture (the tree) to 70% of its original size, while keeping it in proportion, click the image to select it.
    Point to the bottom right handle on the picture then drag it inwards until you can see **70% X 70%** in the **Name Box** on the left of the formula bar.

    To move the picture to cell **E2**, drag the picture into cell **E2**.

    To move the WordArt object (Furniture World) up so that the table's title can be clearly seen, click the WordArt object then drag it to the top of the worksheet (near cell B3).

5. To select the WordArt object (Furniture World) and the picture (the tree), click the WordArt object, hold down the ⌈Shift⌋ key and click the picture. To deselect the objects, click elsewhere on the worksheet.

6. To apply a yellow colour to the border of the WordArt object (Furniture World), click the WordArt object to select it.

   Open the list on the [🖉▾] tool button on the **Drawing** toolbar and click yellow.

   To apply black to the text box border and red to the text inside it, click the text box border to select it (make sure the text box border is made up of dots and not hatched lines).

   Open the list on the [▬🖉▾] tool button and click black.

   Open the list on the [A▾] tool button and click red.

7. To delete the picture (the tree), click the picture to select it then press the [Del] key.

SUMMARY EXERCISES

Summary 1   WORKBOOKS AND WORKSHEETS 242

Summary 2   ROWS, COLUMNS AND CELLS.. 243

Summary 3   MANAGING DATA... 244

Summary 4   CALCULATIONS 245

Summary 5   PRESENTATION OF DATA 246

Summary 6   PRINTING 248

Summary 7   DRAWING OBJECTS 249

SUMMARY EXERCISES

Summary exercise 1   WORKBOOKS AND WORKSHEETS

Open the **Chess club.xls** workbook in the **Summary** folder in the **MOUS Excel 2002** folder.

Give the name **Total** to **Sheet 3**.

Delete the **LEEDS** worksheet then move the **ABERDEEN** worksheet after the **LONDON** worksheet.

Save the changes you have made to the **Chess club.xls** workbook then close it.

A solution is saved under the name **Solution 1.xls** in the **Summary** folder.

Open the **STONES LTD customers.xls** workbook that is in the **Summary** folder of the **MOUS Excel 2002** folder, then modify the **Customers** worksheet as follows:

	A	B	C	D	E	F	G	I
1				**CUSTOMER LIST**				
2								
3								
4								
5								
6								
7	Code	Name	Surname	Address	City	Postcode	Married	
8	ADA001	Gordon	Adams	30 Lakeside	Port Free	6530	YES	
9	AMO001	Jane	Amos	10 Memorial Drive	Indian Hill	8630	NO	
10	AND001	Jane	Anderson	17 Abbey Crescent	St Lucia	5235	YES	
11	ASK001	Fred	Askett	19 River Lane	Killybill	9520	NO	
12	BAR001	James	Barnett	21 Oak Street	Fern Grove	4120	YES	
13	BAR002	Julian	Barton	22 Harrison Avenue	Greerton	7520	YES	
14	EDW001	John	Edwards	77 Cannon Street	Westport	4101	YES	
15	EVA001	Ben	Evans	91 Headland Walk	Abbeyville	8625	YES	
16	FAI001	Amanda	Fairchilde	103 Westwood Avenue	Port Free	6530	NO	
17	FIE001	Kay	Fielding	60 The Crescent	Fern Grove	4120	YES	
18	GRA001	Melissa	Grant	16 River Wynd	Lorton	4280	YES	
19	GRE001	Amy	Green	25 Ridley Street	Indian Hill	8630	YES	
20	GRE002	James	Greene	2 Seaview	Greerton	7520	NO	
21	GRE003	Lola	Green	45 West Road	Gunston	5230	NO	

Insert two rows after row **4**.

Delete rows **14** to **23** as well as column **B**.

Hide column **H**.

Change the width of column **A** to **9** and the height of row **7** to **30**.

Adjust the width of column **G** to fit its contents.

Freeze rows **1** to **7**.

Move cell **D54** in order to insert it between rows **50** and **51**.

A solution is saved under the name **Solution 2.xls** in the **Summary** folder.

Open the **STONES LTD orders.xls** workbook in the **Summary** folder of the **MOUS Excel 2002** folder and fill in the table in the **Jan** worksheet as shown below:

Order number	Customer code	Surname	Week no.	Order total	Sum paid	Sum outstanding
1	MIL001	MILLER	1	3,850	116	3,734.50
2	PIX001	PIXTON	1	2,575	77	
3	MCG001	MCGILL	2	1,185	36	
4	SMI001	SMITHERS	2	1,625	49	
5	LAN001	LANGLEY	2	1,570	47	
6	BAR002	BARTON	3	1,800	54	
7	GRE003	GREEN	4	635	-	
8	RAY001	RAY	4	790	-	
9	WIL001	WILSON	4	4,550	137	

Change the contents of cell **A10** to **Order no.**.

Remove the format from cells **A6** to **B6**.

Copy the contents of cell **G11** to the adjacent cells **G12** to **G19**.

Move the contents of cell **A27** to cell **A24**.

Copy the format of cell **F10** to cell **F23**.

In cell **A25**, insert a hyperlink that will take you to the **Solution 2.xls** workbook. The text for this hyperlink is **Click here to see customer list**.

Copy the contents of cell **G23** to cell **B5** in the **Recap Qtr** worksheet, and establish a link.

A solution is saved under the name **Solution 3.xls** in the **Summary** folder.

Open the **Deliveries.xls** workbook stored in the **Summary** folder of the **MOUS Excel 2002** folder and complete the table in the worksheet **Sheet1** in order to produce the following results:

	A	B	C	D	E	F	G	H
8								
9	**Week no. 47**	North	East	South	West	**TOTAL**	% per driver	Bonus
10	Josh	10	25	30	25	90	6.61%	
11	Connor	15	20	60	16	111	8.15%	10.00
12	Michael	10	10	65	35	120	8.81%	10.00
13	Jack	12	50	70	70	202	14.83%	20.00
14	Tom	20	40	45	42	147	10.79%	10.00
15	Joe	15	15	80	20	130	9.54%	10.00
16	Steven	50	50	50	80	230	16.89%	20.00
17	Max	80	15	20	16	131	9.62%	10.00
18	Jonathan	15	20	40	18	93	6.83%	
19	Peter	20	30	45	13	108	7.93%	10.00
20	TOTAL	247	275	505	335	1,362		
21	Average	25	28	51	34			
22								

Calculate the total deliveries for each area (**B20** to **F20**) and for each driver (**F10** to **F19**).
Calculate the average number of deliveries for each area (**B21** to **E21**).

In cell **G10**, enter a calculation formula that allows you to calculate the percentage of deliveries made by driver **Josh**. Copy this formula for the other drivers (**G11** to **G19**).

In cells **H10** to **H19**, award a bonus of $20 to those drivers who have made 200 or more deliveries, and a bonus of $10 to those drivers who have made 100 or more deliveries. Those drivers who have made less than 100 deliveries will not receive a bonus.

A solution is saved under the name **Solution 4.xls** in the **Summary** folder.

Open the **Accounts.xls** workbook that is in the **Summary** folder in the **MOUS Excel 2002** folder, and modify the **January** worksheet as shown below:

	A	B	C	D	E
1	BUDGET JANUARY 2000				
2					
3					
4					
5		Projected	Actual	%	Difference
6	Income				
7	Net earnings Mr	1,320	1,360	57.87%	40
8	Net earnings Mrs	900	920	39.15%	20
9	Family Allowance	70	70	2.98%	-
10	Total Income	2,290	2,350		60
11	Expenditure				
12	Rent	420	420	17.87%	-
13	Loans	350	350	14.89%	-
14	Taxes	195	195	8.30%	-
15	Insurance	57	57	2.43%	-
16	Electricty	125	110	4.68%	- 15
17	Telephone	55	68	2.89%	13
18	Savings plan	100	80	3.40%	- 20
19	Leisure	128	130	5.53%	2
20	Food & clothing	620	700	29.79%	80
21	School meals	70	70	2.98%	-
22	Transport	90	85	3.62%	- 5
23	Miscellaneous	80	85	3.62%	5
24	Total Expenditure	2,290	2,350		60

To cell **A1**, apply the font **Arial Black**, size **12**, then colour the characters dark blue.

Apply bold to cells **B5** to **E5**, **A10** and **A24**, and underline the contents of cells **A6** and **A11**.

Apply the fill **Gray - 25%** to cells **B5** to **E5**.

Centre the contents of cells **B5** to **E5** vertically and horizontally

Copy the formatting from cell **B5** to cells **A6** and **A11**.

Apply a left indent of 2 characters to the text in cells **A7** to **A9** and cells **A12** to **A23**.

Merge and centre cells **A1** to **E1**.

Apply the **Percentage** format, with **two** decimal places, to cells **D7** to **D9** and **D12** to **D23**.

Create a style called **Label** based on the format of cell **A6** and then apply that style to cell **A24**.

Add borders to the table.

A solution is saved under the name **Solution 5.xls** in the **Summary** folder.

SUMMARY EXERCISES

Summary exercise 6 PRINTING

Open the **STONES LTD customers 2.xls** workbook in the **Summary** folder of the **MOUS Excel 2002** folder and prepare the **Customers** worksheet for printing:

Change the left and right margins to **1 cm** (0.4 inches if that is your measurement unit) and reduce the scale to **95%** of the normal size.

In the right of the header the name of the workbook should be printed, and in the middle of the footer the number of the page, followed by a forward slash then the total number of pages should be printed.

Repeat the titles from row **7** on each page.

Look at the page setup results using the Print Preview.

Print three copies of page **1**, then two copies of the cell range **A8** to **C52**.

A solution is saved under the name **Solution 6.xls** in the **Summary** folder.

Summary exercise 7   DRAWING OBJECTS

Open the **Toys.xls** workbook, found in the **Summary** folder in the **MOUS Excel 2002** folder, then activate the **2001** worksheet.

Create the column chart below from the table:

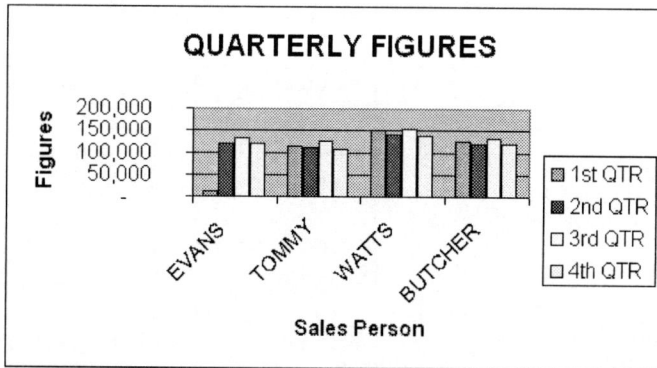

This chart should be inserted as an object underneath the table in the **2001** worksheet; feel free to move and resize the chart.

Carry out the following actions, which will produce the chart in Solution 7:

- Change the size of the font of the labels on the category and value axes to **8**.

- Place the legend under the chart and apply size **9** to the legend text.

- Insert the major gridlines on the category axis.

- Add the **MARSTON** data series to the chart.

Finish the chart by inserting a text box containing the text « Best result » and an arrow, pointing to the largest sales figure.

Print the chart; its size should adjust to fit the page when you print it.

A solution is saved under the name **Solution 7.xls** in the **Summary** folder.

Microsoft Excel 2002 Core Table of objectives 🪟				
Tasks	**Lessons**	**Pages**	**Exercises**	**Pages**
Working with cells and cell data				
Insert, delete and move cells	Lesson 2.2 Titles 6, 7 and 8	57	Exercise 2.2 Points 6, 7 and 8	58
	Lesson 5.1 Title 13	168	Exercise 5.1 Point 13	173
	Lesson 3.3 Titles 2 and 3	99, 100	Exercise 3.3 Points 2 and 3	105
Enter and edit cell data including text, numbers, and formulas	Lesson 3.1 Titles 1 and 6	62 and 72	Exercise 3.1 Points 1 and 6	73 and 74
	Lesson 3.2 Titles 1 and 2	78	Exercise 3.2 Points 1 and 2	91
	Lesson 4.2 Titles 1, 2 and 3	142 to 145	Exercise 4.2 Points 1, 2 and 3	149
	Lesson 5.1 Titles 4 and 5	158 and 160	Exercise 5.1 Points 4 and 5	172
Check spelling	Lesson 3.2 Title 7	88	Exercise 3.2 Point 7	92
Find and replace cell data and formats	Lesson 2.2 Title 4	55	Exercise 2.2 Point 4	58
	Lesson 3.2 Title 6	86	Exercise 3.2 Point 6	91
Work with a subset of data by filtering lists	Lesson 3.4 Titles 1, 2 and 3	110 to 112	Exercise 3.4 Points 1, 2 and 3	113

Tasks	Lessons	Pages	Exercises	Pages
Managing workbooks				
Manage workbook files and folders	Lesson 1.1 Titles 1, 7 and 8	14, 21, 22	Exercise 1.1 Points 1, 7 and 8	28
Create workbooks using templates	Lesson 1.1 Title 4	17	Exercise 1.1 Point 4	28
Save workbooks using different names and file formats	Lesson 1.1 Titles 1 and 6	14 and 21	Exercise 1.1 Points 1 and 6	28
Formatting and printing worksheets				
Apply and modify cell formats	Lesson 5.1 Titles 1, 2 and 3	156 and 157	Exercise 5.1 Points 1, 2 and 3	172
Modify row and column settings	Lesson 2.1 Titles 2, 3, 4, 5	44 to 46	Exercise 2.1 Points 2, 3, 4, 5	49
Modify row and column formats	Lesson 2.1 Title 6	47	Exercise 2.1 Point 6	49
	Lesson 5.1 Titles 6 and 7	160 and 161	Exercise 5.1 Points 6 and 7	172
Apply styles	Lesson 5.2 Title 2	179	Exercise 5.2 Point 2	181
Use automated tools to format worksheets	Lesson 5.1 Title 9	162	Exercise 5.1 Point 9	173
Modify Page Setup options for worksheets	Lesson 6.2 Titles 1, 2 and 3	194 to 199	Exercise 6.2 Points 1, 2 and 3	200
Preview and print worksheets and workbooks	Lesson 6.1 Titles 1, 2, 3, 4	184 to 186	Exercise 6.1 Points 1, 2, 3, 4	190
Modifying workbooks				
Insert and delete worksheets	Lesson 1.2 Titles 8 and 9	38	Exercise 1.2 Points 8 and 9	40
Modify worksheet names and positions	Lesson 1.2 Titles 3, 4 and 5	35 and 36	Exercise 1.2 Points 3, 4 and 5	39

Tasks	Lessons	Pages	Exercises	Pages
Use 3-D references	Lesson 4.2 Title 6	148	Exercise 4.2 Point 6	150
Creating and revising formulas				
Create and revise formulas	Lesson 4.1 Titles 1, 2, 3, 4	132 to 136	Exercise 4.1 Points 1, 2, 3, 4	138
	Lesson 4.2 Titles 1 and 2	142 and 143	Exercise 4.2 Points 1 and 2	149
Use statistical, date and time, financial, and logical functions in formulas	Lesson 4.1 Title 3	134	Exercise 4.1 Point 3	138
	Lesson 4.2 Titles 1, 3, 4, 5	142, 145 to 147	Exercise 4.2 Points 1, 3, 4, 5	149 and 150
Creating and modifying graphics				
Create, modify, position and print charts	Lesson 7.1 Titles 1 to 13	204 to 217	Exercise 7.1 Points 1 to 13	219 and 220
Create, modify and position graphics	Lesson 7.2 Titles 1 to 4, 6 and 7	224 to 235	Exercise 7.2 Points 1 to 4, 6 and 7	236 and 237
Workgroup collaboration				
Convert worksheets into web pages	Lesson 1.1 Titles 9 and 10	22 to 27	Exercise 1.1 Points 9 and 10	29
	Lesson 6.1 Title 5	188	Exercise 6.1 Point 5	190
Create hyperlinks	Lesson 3.1 Title 5	69	Exercise 3.1 Point 5	73
View and edit comments	Lesson 3.5 Title 2	122	Exercise 3.5 Point 2	127

A

ABSOLUTE REFERENCE

Creating   136

ADJUSTING

Columns/rows to fit contents   48

ALIGNING

Cell contents (horizontal)   160
Cell contents (vertical)   161
Indenting text in a cell   170

AUTOFORMAT

Applying to a table   162

AUTOSUM

Using to add cells   134

B

BORDER

Applying to cells   163
Drawing around cells   165

C

CALCULATION

Absolute cell references
in a formula   136
AutoSum   134
Changing calculation mode   133
Copying results   102
Creating a formula   132
Making calculations
on date type data   147
Modifying formulas   134
Using PMT function   146
Using simple statistical functions 142
Using values from different
sheets   72
See also FORMULA, FUNCTION

CATEGORY

Adding to a chart   217
Deleting from a chart   217

CELL

Aligning contents horizontally   160
Aligning contents vertically   161
Clearing contents   78
Clearing formatting   78
Deleting   57
Moving between cells   34
Going to a specific cell   55
Inserting empty cells   57
Merging   168

Modifying borders   163
Modifying contents   78
Moving then inserting   57
Selecting (adjacent)   54
Selecting (non-adjacent)   54
Selecting according to content   56
See also ENTERING DATA

CHART

Activating/deactivating   209
Adding a data category   217
Adding a data series   216
Changing type   212
Creating   204
Deleting a data category   217
Deleting a data series   215
Gridlines   213
Legend   215
Modifying tick mark labels   214
Page setup   207
Previewing   208
Printing   209
Selecting chart objects   210

CLIP ART

Finding and inserting   227
Using the Clip Organizer   231

CLIP ORGANIZER

Using   231

COLOUR

Colouring a sheet tab   36
Colouring cell background   167
Font colour   157

COLUMN

Adjusting width to contents   48
Deleting   45
Freezing/unfreezing   46
Hiding   46
Inserting   44
Modifying width   47
Repeating titles on each page   199
Selecting   44

COMMENT

Filtering discussion comments   126
Managing in Web discussions   123
Replying to a discussion
comment   125
See also WEB DISCUSSIONS

COPYING

Calculation results and formats   102
Cell contents to adjacent cells   98
Cells   99
Excel data into another
application   103
Formats   162
Linking cells during copying   104
Multiple items   100
Sheet in a workbook   36
Sheet into another workbook   37
Transposing data while copying   103
See also MOVING

D

DATA

*See CALCULATION, CELL,
ENTERING DATA*

DATA SERIES

Adding to a chart	216
Creating	66
Creating a custom series	68
Deleting from a chart	215

DATABASE

See LIST

DATE

Entering	62
Entering the system date	65
Formatting	160
Making calculations on date type data	147

DELETING

Cell contents	78
Cells	57
Drawing object	235
Rows/columns	45
Sheets	38

DIAGRAM

Inserting	225

DISCUSSIONS

See WEB DISCUSSIONS

DRAWING OBJECT

Changing a 2D object's appearance	234
Changing a 3D object's appearance	235
Creating	224
Creating a text box	226
Deleting	235
Resizing/moving	233
Selecting	234

E

ENTERING DATA

Copying cell contents	98
Entering the system date	65
Several lines of text in one line	65
Text, values, dates	62

F

FILE

Choosing the default file location	22
See also WORKBOOK	

FILTER

Creating and using a simple filter	110
Filtering by a field value	110
Filtering by a specific criterion	110
Filtering by two criteria for the same field	112
Filtering discussion comments	126
Filtering the highest and lowest values	111
Showing all records	112

FINDING

Cell by its formatting	81
Cell with a particular content	79
Files/items/Web page (advanced search)	84
Files/items/Web pages	82
Replacing contents/formats	86

FOLDER

Creating a folder	21

FONT

Modifying character font	156

FOOTER

See *HEADER/FOOTER*

FORMAT

Applying cell borders	163
Applying patterns to cells	167
AutoFormat	162
Clearing cell formatting	78
Colouring cells	167
Copying	102
Copying formatting	162
Dates/times	160
Indenting text	170
Numerical values	158
Replacing formatting	87
Text attributes	157

FORMAT PAINTER

Using to copy formats	162

FORMULA

Changing calculation mode	133
Creating	132
Including absolute cell references	136
Modifying	134
Using 3D references	148

FREEZING

Rows/columns	46

FUNCTION

Inserting manually	145
Inserting with help from Excel	143
Using PMT function	146
Using simple statistical functions	142

G

GRIDLINES

Adding to chart   213
Printing cell gridlines   195

H

HEADER/FOOTER

Creating   197

HIDING

Rows and columns   46

HYPERLINK

Creating to a place
in a workbook   70
Creating towards a file/
Web page   69

I

INDENTING

Text in a cell   170

INSERTING

Column   44
Diagram   225
Empty cells   57
Function   143
Function manually   145
Moving and inserting cells   57
Rows   44
Sheets   38
Symbols   64
WordArt object   224

INTERNET

See *WEB DISCUSSIONS,
WEB PAGE*

L

LINE

Entering several lines of text
in one cell   65

LINK

Establishing between cells
while copying   103
Linking to a discussion server 116

LIST

Creating a simple filter   110
Filtering by a criterion   110
Filtering by one field value   110

Filtering with multiple criteria   112

M

MARGIN

Defining   196

MERGING

Cells   168

MOVING

Cells   99
Cells and inserting them   57
Drawing object   233
Finding a cell by its contents   56
From one sheet to another   35
Going to a particular cell   34
Going to a specific cell   55
Multiple items   100
Sheet to another workbook   37
With the Office clipboard   100
Within a worksheet   34
Worksheet   36

N

NAME

Naming a sheet   35

O

OBJECT

See DRAWING OBJECT

OFFICE CLIPBOARD

Using to copy/move
multiple items   100

ONLINE DISCUSSIONS

See WEB DISCUSSIONS

OPENING

Choosing the default
file location   22
Shared document   122
Workbook   14

ORIENTATION

Changing text orientation   169
Modifying page orientation   194

P

PAGE

Repeating titles on each page   199

PAGE SETUP

Accessing options 194
Changing the scale of printed
pages 195
Creating page headers
and footers 197
Defining page setup for a chart 207
Defining printing margins 196
Modifying page orientation 194
Repeating titles on each page 199
See also PRINTING

PASTE OPTIONS

Using the Paste Options button 102

PATTERN

Applying to cell background 167

PICTURE

Inserting 227

PMT

Using PMT function 146

PREVIEW

Previewing a chart before
printing 208
Previewing a non-interactive
Web page . 188
Web Page Preview 27

PRINT AREA

Creating 184

PRINT PREVIEW

Previewing a sheet
before printing 186

PRINTING

Cell gridlines 195
Chart 209
Comments and/or formula
errors 196
Margins 196
Modifying the page setup
options 194
Previewing a chart before
printing 208
Previewing a sheet before
printing 186
Printing scale 195
Repeating titles on each page 199
Row and column headings 195
Setting the print options 185
Using a print area 184
Workbook 184
See also PAGE SETUP

R

REPLACING

Cell contents/formats 86

RESIZING

Drawing object 233

ROW

Adjusting height to contents	48
Deleting	45
Freezing/unfreezing	46
Hiding	46
Inserting	44
Modifying height	47
Repeating titles on each page	199
Selecting	44

S

SAVING

Choosing the default file location	22
Existing workbook	20
New workbook	19
Workbook under another name	21
Worksheet/workbook as a Web page	22

SCALE

Printing scale	195

SEARCH

See *FINDING*

SELECTING

Adjacent cells	54
All cells	55
Cells according to content	56
Drawing object	234
Non-adjacent cells	54

Rows and columns	44

SHAREPOINT

Using for online discussions	116

See also *WEB DISCUSSIONS*

SHARING

Creating a shared document for a team	120
Data through a Web site	116
Opening a shared document	122

SHOWING

Hidden rows and columns	46

SIZE

Modifying character size	156

See also *RESIZING*

SOUND

Inserting	227

SPELLING

Checking	88

STATISTICS

Using simple statistical functions	142

STYLE

Applying	179
Creating	178
Integrating styles from another workbook	180

Modifying/deleting 179

SUM

Using AutoSum 134

SYMBOL

Inserting 64

T

TAB

Changing colour of a sheet tab 36

TASK PANE

Using the Advanced
Search pane 84
Using the Basic Search pane 82
Using the Clipboard pane 100
Using the Insert Clip Art pane 227

TEMPLATE

Creating a workbook
from a template 17

TEXT

Checking spelling 88
Entering 62
Indenting in a cell 170
Modifying orientation 169
Replacing with another 86
See also ENTERING DATA

TEXT BOX

Creating 226

3D REFERENCE

Using in formulas 148

TICK MARKS

Modifying labels 214

TIME

Formatting 160

TRANSPOSING

While copying data 103

V

VALUE

Entering 62

VIDEO

Inserting 227

W

WEB DISCUSSIONS

Closing/reopening discussions 125
Creating a shared document
for a team 120
Creating a shortcut
to a team Web site 119
Creating comments 123
Deleting comments 123
Filtering discussion comments 126
Linking to a server 116
Modifying comments 123
Opening a shared document 122
Replying to a discussion
comment 125

WEB PAGE

Creating a hyperlink 69
Finding 82
Previewing a non-interactive
Web page 188
Previewing in Excel 27
Saving a non-interactive
Web page 22
Saving an interactive Web page 24

WEB SITE

Creating a shortcut
to a team Web site 119
Using a team Web site 116
See also WEB DISCUSSIONS

WINDOW

Freezing/unfreezing panes 46

WORD ART

Inserting 224

WORKBOOK

Created from a template 17
Creating 17
Displaying/hiding an open
workbook 17
Opening 14
Printing 184
Saving 19
Saving a non-interactive
Web page 22
Saving an interactive Web page 24
Saving under another name 21

WORKSHEET

Changing tab colour 36
Copying into a workbook 36
Deleting 38
Going from one sheet to another 35
Inserting 38
Moving 36
Moving around within cells 34
Moving/copying into another
workbook 37
Naming 35
Saving a non-interactive
Web page 22
Saving an interactive Web page 24
Selecting all cells 55

List of available titles in
the Microsoft Office User Specialist collection

Visit our Internet site for the list of the latest titles published.
http://www.eni-publishing.com

ACCESS 2002
ACCESS 2000
EXCEL 2000 CORE
EXCEL 2000 EXPERT
EXCEL 2002 CORE
EXCEL 2002 EXPERT
OUTLOOK 2000
OUTLOOK 2002
POWERPOINT 2000
POWERPOINT 2002
WORD 2000 CORE
WORD 2000 EXPERT
WORD 2002 CORE
WORD 2002 EXPERT